From Raymond Edwards Philip

The Elijah Syndrome

How One Minister Deals with a Bipolar Condition

RAYMOND FRANKLIN EDWARDS,
BA, MDIV

ISBN 978-1-64670-385-2 (Paperback)
ISBN 978-1-64670-386-9 (Digital)

Scriptures are taken from the
HOLMAN CHRISTIAN STANDARD BIBLE®
(unless otherwise noted)
Copyright © 1999–2018
Holman Bible Publishers

Scriptures designated (NCV) are taken from New Century Version, copyright © 1987, 1988, 1991, By Word Publishing, a division of Thomas Nelson. Inc. Used by permission

Scriptures designated (NIV) are taken from HOLY BIBLE, NEW INTERNATIONAL VERSION. Copyright © 1973, 1978, 1984 International Bible Society.
Used by permission of Zondervan Bible Publishers.

Scriptures designated (NKJV) are taken from the New King James Version©. Copyright © 1982 By Thomas Nelson. Used by permission. All rights reserved.

Covenant Books, Inc.
11661 Hwy 707
Murrells Inlet, SC 29576
www.covenantbooks.com

Dedication and Acknowledgment

Without hesitation I dedicate this work to my wife and kids. I do so with a very clear reason.

First, my wife, Marie, has been with me for over fifty-four years. She has been a caregiver, advisor, trusted critic, confidant, faithful wife, and mother. While doing all the above she has been on the move so many times, and has lived in all kinds of apartments, houses, duplexes, trailers, mobile homes, and assorted domiciles. I know that Marie has had her times of disappoint, sadness, and hurt. I have not always been the best of caregiver to her. But Marie is strong in her prayer life. I could not have designed a greater ministry partner than Marie. Thank you, Lord, for my wife.

Secondly, I dedicate this book to my daughter Angela and my son Anthony. I know it was not an easy role model, having a father as a Gospel minister. I love both of you so very much. If I had known back then, while you were still at home, some positive principles of fatherhood I have learned later, I am sure I would have been a better father. I want to thank Angela for her continued positive criticism as I have worked on this book.

Finally, I wish to acknowledge, Dr. Donnie Joe Holden, my psychiatrist. He is the one who planted in my mind and heart a book such as this. He challenged me to author such a book. Without his encouragement, this book might have never been a reality.

Raymond Franklin Edwards, 2019

CONTENTS

FOREWORD

If you really want to know what war is like, don't seek someone who has only heard about it. Go to a combat veteran and ask this person to tell you the truth. If you can even get the person (he or she) to talk about what was experienced, you will get the unvarnished reality. And then, only then, will you get as close as you possibly can to knowing what, in all actuality, war is.

If you want to know what it is like to live with a mental or emotional ailment, you must use the same tactic. Most people, like soldiers who've been at the frontlines, have little desire to talk about it to others outside the close (and perhaps closed) circle of family, physicians, counselors, and therapy groups. To some, it's embarrassing. To others, the fear of misunderstanding and/or rejection takes control. And to still more people, it seems to highlight perceived weakness. However, if a courageous soul steps up to share his or her story, we are always better for it. (It may be the same for them too.)

The book you are about to read is important for just such a reason.

It will be enlightening.

It will be insightful.

It will be biblical.

It will be worth it.

You will come away with a new appreciation for those who battle every day with what is not easily understood. Your understanding of scripture will be increased, and Bible characters will allow you to gain perspective on their struggles—and maybe yours.

Your guide will be a man for whom I have great respect and admiration. I'm honored to be his pastor and privileged to be his friend. Oh, and he is the person well equipped to teach you what you need to know about mental distress. Ray Edwards has been used mightily of the Lord over several decades as pastor, teacher, missionary, and, now, church member. All the while, he served with bouts of depression, eventually being diagnosed with bipolar disorder. This book, his story, is written with compassion for all and heart for God's people.

Having worked in the public mental health field and served churches in different capacities, I knew of the need for *this* book. I wish it had been written years ago. But God had reserved it for such a time as this. Maybe it's just for you because now is the time you need it and will read it. It might be about you, or a loved one, or the church you serve.

Significant is a word that I would use as a description for Ray's work. I believe you will agree.

Rob Davis, MRE, MA
Senior Pastor
First Baptist Church
Harrison, Arkansas

INTRODUCTION

Have you ever felt like you were in a hole you could not get out of and the more you struggled to get out, the deeper the hole became? Yes, so have I.

Have thoughts about ending your life raced through your mind and you struggled to stop them, but they were so powerful you felt almost overwhelmed by them? Yes, so have I.

Have you ever curled up in a fetal position in your bed in the middle of the day with the curtains drawn and the lights off and lay there for hours? Yes, so have I.

Have you ever tried to hurt yourself in some way because you thought the pain would still be less than the one you were feeling inside? Yes, so have I.

Have you ever wanted to run away and perhaps change your name, go where no one knew you, and start a new life in some far-away place? Yes, so have I.

Have you ever wanted to just once give in to your darkest urges and hope no one would ever know? Yes, so have I.

If you have experienced any, some, all, or even other things like these, this book is for you.

Maybe your experience is like the following:

"Honey, I'm not going to church today."

"Why not?" the wife inquired.

"Because I'm depressed, I'm not appreciated, my service in that church does not seem to count for anything, I simply feel tired and used up."

"But, dear," pleaded the wife, "you must go, you have to go."

"Why must I go? Why do I have to go?"

"Because, dear, you're the pastor!"

You may be a pastor, or Christian minister of one sort or another, or even the leader of some secular enterprise and your life is about to become an emotional tragedy. You may have just experienced an emotional burnout. You may have just stepped away from the work because of symptoms of depression or similar psychological or emotional episodes. You may have been diagnosed with chronic depression or a bipolar condition (formerly called manic-depressive disorder). Or you may be one of thousands of laymen or laywomen who suffer from various types of depressive emotional problems that make it difficult to live a normal life. If so, this book is for you.

I was ordained a Southern Baptist Minister in 1965. In 2008, I was diagnosed with a bipolar condition. I have pastored churches, started churches, and been involved in missions work in many countries of the world. I have preached scores of revivals and conducted various types of Bible conferences. I have been involved in organizing and teaching seminary extension and taught as adjunct professor for two different colleges. But all these experiences still did not totally prepare me for the diagnosis I received in 2008.

Let me affirm this truth: God is still on His throne and the calling He placed on my life still stands. Yes, I have a brain disorder, and like Paul, it seems that God has chosen not to remove this particular thorn, so He gives daily grace to live with it. My psychiatrist, who is a fine Christian, encouraged me to write this book. I am not a talented writer, so it has been a labor of love. My prayer is that this work will give you a measure of hope, help, and a handle on some of your problems and challenges.

Note to the Reader

Elijah was perhaps the greatest prophet of the Old Testament. The Hebrew people revered him as such, yet the book of James tells us he was still a man with weaknesses, not so different from many of us today. In chapter 6, I deal at length with the experience of Elijah the prophet and his experience on Mt. Carmel as he faces the prophets of Baal. His experience and subsequent reaction provide an interesting analogy of a bipolar episode. I am not implying that Elijah was bipolar, but there are valuable lessons we can draw from the event. He does exhibit many of the classic symptoms of a bipolar condition.

First Kings 18–19 is the Biblical material we draw from with an additional comment from James 5:17–18. As you read, chapter 6 you will understand my reason for entitling this book *The Elijah Syndrome*.

Please read this before going any farther. The advice I share in the following pages comes from my personal experience, my own research, my study of scripture, and my walk with God over many years. I do not claim to have any special training in the field of medicine, psychiatry, psychotherapy, genetics, nutrition, or bodily exercise. The suggestions and recommendations I share have helped me. And it is my prayer that given the chance, they will help you, especially those that are grounded in the Word of God.

Part I

My Story and Learning about Being Bipolar

1

FINDING OUT I
HAD A PROBLEM

I was reared in a Christian home. My family was active in a little Southern Baptist Church in rural northern Arkansas. I had one sibling, a sister five years younger than me. I surrendered my life to the Lord Jesus Christ when I was sixteen years old. I made a commitment to become a Gospel minister when I was eighteen years old.

There was nothing particularly unique about my childhood. I grew up on a small farm, like most of those I went to school with. I was a very shy kid but socialized well enough. I did not do well at team sports and was always chosen last to be on any team we happened to be forming. I guess that bothered me more than I realized at the time.

Years later, far into adulthood, when I was helping organize a baseball or softball game, my hands would sweat; and for a few moments, I was that little boy being chosen last for the team. Many people experience those psychosomatic reactions, but I am sure I made more of them than I should have. It was not so much a problem of poor self-image but a failure to understand how God sees me in Christ's image. I see that now in hindsight.

I was ordained to the ministry at nineteen years of age while pastoring my first church. It was New Hope Baptist Church on Arkansas Highway 14, just a few miles out of Yellville, Arkansas. That same year, 1965, I married Anna Marie Estes, after which we moved to Walnut Ridge, Arkansas, to attend college. There I began pastoring my second church, Light Baptist Church, between Walnut

Ridge and Paragould. Let me be honest, I was ill prepared to be a pastor, but God was gracious and the people were patient.

After finishing junior college at Southern Baptist College, Walnut Ridge, Arkansas, we moved to Bolivar, Missouri, where Marie and I enrolled in Southwest Baptist College. The years between 1967 and 1969 were quite eventful. I pastored two more student churches. The first church was Pine Creek Baptist, which was about seventy miles east of Bolivar. We enjoyed our weekend trips and our time of fellowship with that wonderful country congregation. Our second church was Osage Baptist, in Carroll County, Arkansas, which was close to our home; and they had the added benefit of a small parsonage. We felt we might remain there for a while after I graduated. It was a great group of folks who were deeply spiritual. But our stay there was shorter than we anticipated.

We lost our first child shortly after birth, and Marie had to drop out of school. Another baby was born in October 1969, Angela Darlene. God gave us comfort and direction as it was needed. He gave us friends we could lean on. God was very good to us. I graduated in the summer of 1969 with a bachelor of arts degree, a double major in history and Christianity. I had a minor in psychology. Marie was able to complete approximately eighty hours of college work but did not receive a degree.

In December 1969, we moved to Albany, Oregon, where I began pastoring Calvary Baptist Church. (Angela was six weeks old.) With college behind us, this was our first opportunity to settle into a normal routine as a pastor's family.

We jumped into our ministry at Calvary Baptist Church, Albany, Oregon, with much anticipation. We enjoyed the challenge of a pioneer area for evangelicals. I think this is where I first began to have a heart for missions.

But I also began to discover some things about myself I was not aware of: (1) I was not a good manager of money; I did not use credit wisely. (2) I was impatient; I wanted things to happen before they had time to develop. (3) I was very inconsiderate of my wife and was very selfish as a husband. (4) My church came before my family. (5) I was extremely moody and did not know how to be constructive with my moods. (6) I was great at starting projects but poor at finishing them. (7) And I was not very good at delegating. It was not a pretty picture. (By the way, I was a decent preacher, teacher, personal worker, and evangelist.)

I am afraid the negative outweighed the positive, and there were repercussions. One night I came home to find my wife in tears.

"What is wrong?" I inquired.

I was thinking, *Your man is here and whatever is wrong, I can fix it! I'm Mr. Fix It!*

WRONG!

She said, "Ray, I don't have a pastor. You come home every night and dump on me, but who do I dump on? There's nobody for me to go to and share my burden with. I don't have a pastor."

I was totally devastated. We had been having problems. It is not necessary that I detail those problems here. But our marriage had become rather shaky. This seemed to be a final blow. I felt like a failure. During the next few days, I remembered the name of a Christian psychiatrist that a cousin who lived in Salem, Oregon, had told me about. He attended her church and specialized in marriage counseling. We were able to get in touch with him and set up an appointment with Dr. JR for the following week.

Back in those days, there was not a lot of good material written about Christian marriage relationships. But our association with him began a transformation in my relationship toward my wife, my church, and my walk with God. We invited Dr. JR to our church to lead a marriage conference.

As I looked back on those days, I realize I had dealt with some of those negative issues, but not all. I also see now there were hints of a bipolar brain malfunction that would someday manifest itself in a greater way. First, handling money poorly is sometimes a symptom of the manic side of a bipolar condition. Second, starting great and ending poorly is also a symptom of manic behavior. Third, moodiness is a symptom, especially of the depressive side of a bipolar condition.

If I had saved all the money wasted on buying cars (new and used), I would now have a much better retirement income. I would always pray before I bought or traded for a car, and in my mind, it was always "the will of God." Most of the time, it was my bipolar speaking. Please understand, I am not using being bipolar as an excuse for my behavior but as an explanation. In those earlier years, I knew nothing of a bipolar condition or a manic-depressive condition, as it was called back them. I will explain those terms more in detail later in this book.

By the way, before we left Oregon, the church had experienced both numerical growth and growth in spiritual depth. God can still use us even if we are messed up.

I would often explain my short pastorates by using a baseball analogy. I would say that I was a good middle reliever (referring to a baseball pitcher). I would come in and rally the team, see them get several runs ahead, and then move to the next team that needed my services. I have come to realize that my short pastorates were partly a result of my bipolar condition. Please understand, God was using me even in my ignorance. And perhaps God was putting me in churches that were ministering to me as much as I was ministering to them. There is always a divine mystery to how God works these things out. Romans 5:8 is always in play. The "Edwards personal translation" says, "God works all things together for those that truly love the Lord and are divinely called to serve His purposes [even over human weakness]."

Yes, early in my ministry, I knew I had some problems. I was working on the marriage thing. I knew that was a long-term project. Marie and I were committed to making it work. As for the ministry, I felt that four things would surely help me in those other areas:

1. Endeavor to deepen my spiritual life.
2. Become involved in more good projects and organizations.
3. Wait until I had gained more experience.
4. Get more theological education.

As I look back now, I see how patient God was with me. I was so very immature, but I did love the Lord, and I knew He had a call on my life. At the time, I did not know how long it would take and all that God would have to lead me through to start getting me where He wanted me to be. By the way, God is still working on me, but He has brought me far from where I once was. God did begin to deepen my spiritual life, but it was not a result of my endeavor. I did get more involved in area wide and community events. My calendar was full. But what I discovered was that my busyness did not equate to a richer and more joyful life. In fact, it often worked at cross purposes with my responsibility as a husband and father.

As far as experience, we all receive that. The real challenge is learning from them. I must admit that much of the time I was a slow learner. After two and half years in Oregon, we left for Fort Worth, Texas, where I was to attend Southwestern Baptist Theological Seminary. There I was to get my theological training. The story takes a twist in the next chapter.

We arrived in Fort Worth in the early summer of 1972. We were anxious to get settled in seminary housing, and I needed to find a job. I was to start school in the fall. But all was not as it seemed. I had received a letter approving us for seminary housing but had not received a letter accepting me as a student for the fall 1972 semester. When I visited the registrar's office, I was informed that a letter had been sent informing me that I had not been accepted as a student at this time. Apparently, we left Oregon before the letter arrived. The reason we were turned down was because of our financial condition.

Oh, God put us through school but not the one we had planned on attending. In a period of six months, we moved six times. While there, our second child was born, a boy, Anthony Mark. I directed music for a small church south of Fort Worth, and Marie worked as a church secretary.

There was a stubbornness in me that caused me to not want to go back to Arkansas. I worked as a custodian for the Arlington School District. I worked the night shift. I was discouraged and depressed. One night while cleaning in the office area, I simply broke down and began to pour out my heart to God. I said, "Lord, something has to change, I am ready to go anywhere you want me to go. I'll even go back to Arkansas if you want me to. I've got to have peace and direction." Well, it was not long before God began to open a door for us to return to Arkansas. I will not spend time with all the details, but God was continuing to chisel away to make me look more like Jesus.

2

LIVING IN IGNORANCE

It would be a few years before I would return to Southwestern Seminary to complete my MDiv degree. I remember the hunger I had to go to seminary. I somehow felt lacking without it. One of my special mentors, Brother John Finn, one of the godliest men I have ever known, said to me, "Brother Raymond, God has a lot of different ways of educating His preachers." That statement satisfied my heart. So I died to my desire to go to seminary. And as soon as I died to my desire to go to seminary, God said, "I want you to go!"

Before we moved back to Southwestern Seminary and while I was pastoring a small Arkansas country church, I experienced a life-altering event. Years before, I had begun to use the expression "I want to be in on whatever God is up to." I really meant that. I did not know the power of what I was saying.

It was during the Thanksgiving season, and I was going through a very low time in my life. I did not know to call it depression, but I suppose that is what it was. I remember feeling separated from all that was going on around me. Others were happy, and could praise the Lord, but I had to force it. For me it seemed a show; it seemed unreal.

I forced myself to look happy, but I was dying on the inside. I preached sermons about victory but did not feel victorious on the inside. I would go to my little prayer room at the church building and agonize before God to do something in my life, to change things, but I continued to feel empty. Then one day, I prayed a final prayer to God, "Lord, I cannot go on this way any longer. I am desperate for something to change. I am more of a detriment to your kingdom than an asset. If you do not do something soon, I'm just going to quit."

Nothing happened right away. My prayer life simply stopped. I was scheduled to speak in a neighboring city at a joint Thanksgiving celebration. I did not have anything fresh from God, so I pulled a message out of the barrel. It was on a Wednesday night, so I had to be gone from my own church. When I returned, I met one deacon who was just leaving the Wednesday service. He shared with me that the church had conducted a special business meeting, and in his own words, "things were about to blow to pieces." He got into his car and began his drive home.

I stood there for a moment, looked up at that old church building, and said, "Lord, this is your church, not mine, and since you're going to be up all night anyway, I'll let you handle it. I'm going to the parsonage, go to bed, and go to sleep." And that is exactly what I did. The next morning, it hit me—God had answered my prayer! I did not yell, scream, bark like a dog, jump three feet into the air, or shout for two hours (not that I'm necessarily opposed to any of that if God is genuinely leading); but what I did receive was an overwhelming sense of peace that was completely indescribable. I experienced a filling of the Holy Spirit.

Some folks speak about the "baptism of the Holy Spirit," but I believe the biblically correct and less confusing expression would be "one baptism, many fillings." I would have to testify that this filling for me was, up until that time, the most significant.

If you do not receive anything else out of this book, please pay attention here. In Ephesians 5, Paul says something you need to heed:

> See then that you walk circumspectly, not as fools but as wise, redeeming the time, because the days are evil.
>
> Therefore do not be unwise, but understand what the will of the Lord is. And do not be drunk with wine, in which is dissipation; but be filled with the Spirit, speaking to one another in psalms and hymns and spiritual songs, singing

and making melody in your heart to the Lord, giving thanks always for all things to God the Father in the name of our Lord Jesus Christ, submitting to one another in the fear of God. (Eph. 5:15–21 NKJV)

The Holman Christian Standard Bible translates Ephesians 5:15–21 this way:

Pay careful attention, then, to how you walk—not as unwise people but as wise—making the most of the time, because the days are evil. So don't be foolish, but understand what the Lord's will is. And don't get drunk with wine, which leads to reckless actions, but be filled by the Spirit: speaking to one another in psalms, hymns, and spiritual songs, singing and making music from your heart to the Lord, giving thanks always for everything to God the Father in the name of our Lord Jesus Christ, submitting to one another in the fear of Christ.

The first defense against any malady—whether mental, emotional, physical malady, or a demonic—is to be filled with the Holy Spirit. To be filled with the Holy Spirit is to be controlled by the Holy Spirit. A believer is to be being filled. It is a daily process. Since that night outside that little Arkansas church, I have experienced many fillings. I can never get more of God than I received when I first trusted Him by faith and became part of His spiritual family, but God constantly seeks to get more of me. Praise His Name!

Let me briefly point out in the forgoing passage that being controlled by the Holy Spirit is linked to (1) our walk, (2) our wisdom, (3) God's will, (4) our worship of God, (5) and our witness.

Do you want to be controlled by an evil system from without that wants to *destroy* you or an eternal Savior from within that wants to *design* you, *delegate* you, and *deploy* you as a kingdom representative? Satan wants you as a *tool of his grief*, but God has called you to be a *trophy of His grace*.

By the way, nothing was about ready to blow to pieces in that church. And I want to add, by God's grace, He put us in two wonderful churches during a time we needed the kind of people those churches had. We have made lasting and loving relationships from both those congregations. Rock Springs Baptist Church, Eureka Springs, Arkansas, was a church that taught us much about the joy of living the Christian faith. Rosie Baptist Church, Rosie, Arkansas, allowed me to attend Mid-America Seminary in Memphis, Tennessee. Their encouragement led to a greater love for the Word of God. We have been back to both churches many times for various events. We hold many fond memories of our ministry to those congregations.

God had prepared me and my family spiritually to attend seminary. So in the fall of 1977, we left Rosie Baptist Church and moved to Southwestern Baptist Theological Seminary in Fort Worth, Texas. God had constructed a spiritual foundation in our lives that would be put to the test many times, but God knew how strong it needed to be.

It was about halfway through the 1977 fall semester I felt fear creeping in. The spirit of fear is not from the Lord. We had left a place of financial security and had launched out by faith to obey God in moving to seminary. It looked like my outgo was exceeding my income so that my upkeep was going to be my downfall. But I had to learn that God's promises were the great equalizers.

About midnight after returning from work, I bowed at the living room couch and began to complain to God. "Lord, I don't understand, we were doing good before we moved. We were paying our bills, buying groceries, everything was up to date. Now, things look bleak. I don't know how we are going to make it from month to month. What are you up to?"

God said, "*In everything, give thanks for this is the will of God in Christ Jesus.*"

I said, "Lord, I don't feel thankful."

He said, "*In everything, give thanks.*"

I said, "Lord, I'm not very thankful."

He said, "*In everything, give thanks.*"

I said, "Lord, do you want me to give you thanks even when I don't feel thankful?"

He said, "*In everything, give thanks for this is the will of God in Christ Jesus.*"

So that night, I started to give God thanks by faith. "Lord, I praise you in this situation. You are still on the throne. You will make sure our needs are met, our bills are paid, time to study is provided, I will be able to do a good job for my boss, a church position will become available [it did], my life will cross paths with the right people, so on and so forth. I praise you, Lord. I don't know how you are going to do it, but I claim it done in the name of Jesus. I praise you it is done."

I continued to have a glorious worship time with the Lord and learned the value of praising God by faith.

So along with the foundation of being filled with (controlled by) the Holy Spirit, I learned the power of praise. These two foundation stones were essential for me to deal with what I would have to face later when I received my bipolar diagnosis.

I found this anonymous quote recently:

> You need to understand that the enemy is not really after your dreams, your health, or your finances. He's not primarily after your family. He's after your joy. The Bible says, that *"the joy of the LORD is your strength"* (Nehemiah 8:10 NKJV) [emphasis mine], and your enemy knows if he can deceive you into living down in the dumps and depressed, you are not going to have the necessary strength—physically, emotionally, or spiritually—to withstand his attacks.

The scope of this book does not allow me to share a lot of details that might prove helpful in a different context. So I must stay with those experiences that relate to my bipolar diagnosis. Seminary was a very positive experience. We were preparing to go to the foreign mission field. That process was postponed because of some health issues with my Anna Marie. Upon graduating from Southwestern in the summer of 1980, we moved to northern Illinois where we became "church planters" with a commitment of three years.

I jumped into this work like I did every other responsibility I had taken—full speed ahead. I spent one week in the hospital with double pneumonia. I was hospitalized another week for what they thought might have been a heart attack. It was decided, however, that I had pulled a muscle very close to my heart and two heart enzymes were elevated. The muscle pull happened because I had been carrying railroad ties on my shoulder helping landscape property we had purchased for our new church building.

The third medical episode is linked to the title of this chapter. I began to have episodes of crying for no known reason. Both of our children were still rather young. Our son was in grammar school, and our daughter was beginning junior high. Sometimes I would begin to weep because of something the kids would say to me. I was puzzled. I had never experienced anything like this before. So in a moment of brilliance, I began to self-diagnose. I had read about this type of reaction in people who had low blood sugar. I made an appointment with a physician in Joliet, Illinois. He administered the five-hour glucose test. I met with him afterward for the results. The good news was, I had no sugar problem. But what he said next blew me away.

This was my first encounter with this doctor. He was not a practicing Christian but was very respectful of my convictions and of my vocation. He said, "Mr. Edwards, you show all the classic signs of chronic depression." I was speechless. I really did not know how to respond.

What I was feeling inside was, *This is a spiritual matter, and if I am depressed I ought to know it, and I need to go to God to get it fixed.*

The doctor said, "I know you don't drink, or smoke, or do drugs, right?"

"Oh, right."

Then he asked, "What hobbies do you have? What do you do to relax? Do you have a set day a week you take off?"

I mumbled a few words about the YMCA and that my work was my hobby.

Then he looked at me and said, "Mr. Edwards, whether you get better or not is up to you. What are you going to do about it?"

He gave me some literature about depression and sent me home.

I discarded the literature and spent the next several years in ignorance about the nature of depression and other related mental and emotional malfunctions. It probably hastened my own emotional burnout and robbed myself of opportunities to help dozens of hurting people in the churches I pastored. That is my greatest shame. By the way, by the time we left Illinois, we had laid aside the plan to become career foreign missionaries. Time and circumstances would prove that decision a correct one.

I spent the next several years living in denial. If you want to take the opinion that depression and other similar problems are simply spiritual in nature and the cure is to get yourself completely right with God, there is plenty of material out there to support your notion. I tried that route, but I always ended up frustrated. One can even twist the scripture to make a case for that position. What happens is, you will put yourself under greater guilt and if you are counseling someone else with a similar problem, you will put them under greater guilt. It becomes a no-win situation. In my younger years as a minister, I sadly mistook hardheaded stubbornness for standing firm for the truth. But one must know what the truth is before he can take a stand for it.

Misconceptions about Mental Illness

As Christians, we are to love and accept those who are challenged, whether physically or mentally. But mental illness seems to present a more difficult challenge. I think the reason is an illogical amount of fear. Fear causes us to recoil from those who need our help the most. Faith in Christ assures us that He not only set the example for touching others in need but also provides us with the ability to be a blessing to those who may have a mental disorder.

I have found there are usually two general reactions from folks when they discover that I have been diagnosed with a bipolar condition:

1. *Overreaction.* These folks seem to know the answer to my problem. Those answers can range all the way from the need for demonic exorcism to hospitalization and medication. Their analysis ranges from thinking the problem is caused by sin to a genetic condition. The truth is, they do not understand, nor can they provide any encouragement to those affected by a mental disorder or malfunction.

2. *Underreaction.* Some believe the problem is not real at all. They will ask questions like, "Tell me, what is really wrong?" or "What happened to trigger this thing you're going through?" Sometimes they will say, "Just tell me what I can do to help?" or "Hang in there, things are bound to get better." The best one is "You know, we all have our ups and downs!"

As someone living with a "brain malfunction," I have learned to extend grace to those who do not understand. Their negative reaction often comes from a sense of fear and lack of education rather than purposefully trying to offend. Many people with a bipolar disorder have manic episodes, which are temporary. However, there are cases where delusions are constant. We need to be prepared to interact with those who have chronic mental illnesses as well as milder forms.

Here are a few common misconceptions about mental illness (brain malfunctions) and how Christians can respond:

1. *People with mental health conditions are unsafe.* Most people with mental illnesses are peaceful and respectful of other people. According to the Institute of Medicine,

    Although studies suggest a link between mental illnesses and violence, the contribution of people with mental illnesses to overall rates of violence is small, and further, the magnitude of the relationship is greatly exaggerated in the minds of the general population

Within the last few years, we have had an increase in terrorist attacks and mass violence. Whenever these disasters take place, the media is quick to judge the suspects and label them as "mentally disturbed", which is rather inaccurate. In reality, only 3-5% of violent crimes in the U.S. are committed by persons who suffer from a mental illness. (Cheung, "Sanism and the Language of Mental Illness," 2015.)

The unfortunate truth is that individuals with mental illness are *more* likely to be victims of violence than perpetrators. Disorders like depression, borderline personality disorder, and bipolar disorder make sufferers more inclined to inflict self-harm than to harm another person. You have no need to fear a person with a mental illness just because of their diagnosis.[1]

When the news reports a mentally ill person being violent, consider how you would feel if you had a mental illness and you had never been violent but were lumped into the same category with those who were violent. How would you react to those who subscribe to a culture of fear?

2. *People with mental illnesses are unpredictable and difficult to relate to.* I know many people who have professional jobs, raise stable families, and live with a mental illness. When someone is unwell, they may become unpredictable. This is not their normal way of interacting, and many people with mental illnesses have a plan in case they become unwell— for example, informing a family member and adjusting their medications.

Give someone the benefit of the doubt, assume they will be dependable, show up to meetings, and relate well. Extend grace and understanding when they are struggling with their mental health. Some people with mental illnesses may have trouble relating to others. Embrace the challenge of interacting with a human being who may have had more struggles in life than you.

3. *Most people with mental illness are usually on welfare or homeless.* Most people with mental illnesses are not homeless. However, as this article from *The Washington Post* points out, "Because the relatively small number of people living on the streets who suffer from paranoia, delusions and other mental disorders are very visible, they have come to stand for the entire homeless population, despite the fact that they are in the minority."[2]

   If homeless people come to our churches, it is especially important to reach out to them. Treat them as equals and have a genuine conversation with them rather than migrating only to people you're comfortable with.

4. *People with mental illnesses would rather not talk about it.* It is surprising how open people can be about their mental health journey. One woman I met in church told me she had a mental illness and shared her experience of discrimination because of it.

   This conversation depends on the person; some people are very open, and others are private. You may find you are blessed with more awareness when you listen to the struggles of someone with a mental illness. Respect where the person is with their ability to share and be open to hearing their mental health struggles.

3

My Diagnosis

After leaving Illinois in 1984 we returned to Arkansas. We began pastoring at First Baptist Church, Lead Hill. Although we were there for only a little over a year, it was a time for us to get some specific direction from the Lord about our future. Our intent was not to stay such a short time, but that is how it seemed to play out. I must say, it was a very exciting and positive year, as far as a relationship with the church. We have been invited back many times for various events. It was from there I took my first overseas mission trip.

I do not recall any obvious symptom of a bipolar problem while there, although I do recall some family conflict and uncertainty. It was not a particularly happy year for the kids. Maybe my inability to make good decisions and stick with them contributed to the sense of uncertainty within the family.

In 1985, we moved to Lyttleton Baptist Church, Manchester, Kentucky. I was pastor there through December 1989. It was the most spiritually productive church I had ever pastored. There were six folks waiting to be baptized when I arrived. The first year, we baptized sixty-five.

Our Sunday morning services were packed out almost every week. The church had dozens of very active witnesses. Folks really took their Christianity seriously. I was challenged to do my best preaching and my best work as pastor. I also made several more foreign mission trips. Though I could not put my finger on it, I felt at times some dark, emotional clouds come over me. Some at the time I attributed to family crises, but now I am not sure they were all domestic situations. I experienced a few panic attacks but never followed up on them. The people of Lyttleton were truly a blessing.

I resigned from Lyttleton Baptist Church after I sensed there was a need for a change in leadership, and we felt a desire to be closer to our aging parents back in Arkansas.

My diagnosis came as more of a process than simply an objective medical determination. We moved from Kentucky in January 1990 to First Baptist Church, Berryville, Arkansas, where we had a very successful pastorate. We moved into a nice parsonage and began to work with a pleasant group of church folks. I had a wonderful time ministering with Richard Metts, our minister of music and youth. Although I was there only a short time, we experienced very few church problems. We even established a mission church close to Eureka Springs, Arkansas. I enjoyed preaching and teaching there. The people were very appreciative and responsive. I was also involved in leading several mission trips with some of my people.

But on a personal level, things were different. My people did not know what was going on inside my head. After less than a year, I remember often waking on Sunday morning wishing I was somewhere else. I would push against those thoughts and go on to church services and preach the sermon I had prepared.

Most of the time, the day went great. But often the next Sunday was a repeat of the week before. It became a very tiring routine, to say the least.

At some point, I began to develop a ringing in my ears. An examination showed I was losing my ability to hear higher frequencies. Sometime after that, I began having panic attacks. If you have never experienced a panic attack, the best way for me to define it is being *illogically fearful* of something that you cannot describe. One night my panic attack was so severe, Marie took me to the hospital for a shot to calm me down.

It was during the approximately two and a half years at Berryville that I am sure now I experienced more of the manic side of my bipolar condition. Not only have I had trouble handling money well, I also have had a weakness for cars. One day, I went to the Dodge dealership and bought a beautiful lease-model Chrysler, completely loaded. I went back to the church and announced to Marie, who was the church secretary at the time, "Guess what? I bought you a new car!"

"You what?"

"I bought you a new car, but it's okay, because I prayed about it, and I really believe the Lord is in this."

Now, this sort of thing did not happen just once. It happened many times. No, not as big a ticket item as a car, but other purchases that were very questionable.

Please hear me. Bipolar is never an excuse for bad behavior, but it can help to explain why we often feel led to do certain things. I had let my manic brain malfunction control me.

After about two years at Berryville, I begin to consider going into vocational evangelism. In a matter of months, I had formed the Ray Edwards Evangelistic Association and became a 501C3 organization. I resigned from the church in April 1992 and moved into a mobile home provided by one of the church families.

Again, I had fallen back into a pattern of acting without a lot of planning or forethought. I think part of my haste to leave the church was trying to run away from my problem. I did stay very busy for the first year and six months. The whole process had taken quite a toll on my wife. I had not sought the advice of my wife. I had not even sat down and discussed with her the pros and cons of leaving the church and the absence of a weekly paycheck. I had not mentioned that going into evangelism meant no specific guarantees of how much money would be coming in and when it would be coming in, and yet she would be responsible for paying the bills. Only God's grace kept that woman with me. As I look back on those times now, I see how badly I treated her and how inconsiderate I was of her needs and feelings.

As my opportunities to do evangelistic events began to diminish, the simple need for a steady income pointed me back to the pastorate. This time I felt, however, I would be better suited and the churches better served if I went in as an interim pastor. But that was not to be. I began pastoring a mission church in Green Forest, Arkansas, which lasted for seven years, the longest I had served anywhere.

Many wonderful things happened at Beth'el Baptist, including a fire which destroyed our portable sanctuary. We built a new one complete with classrooms, kitchen, offices, dining room, nursery, and all without a cross word or argument. The church doubled my salary. We saw dozens of folks receive Jesus Christ as their personal Savior. We had a great youth and children's ministry.

But for me, I knew I had a problem with depression. My emotional reservoir was beginning to empty out. My personal doctor was a member of the church I had served in Berryville. He started me on a mild antidepressant. He also advised us to leave town for at least two weeks. We went to the Florida Panhandle. After a couple of panic attacks, I settled down and relaxed for a few days. But during those seven years at Beth'el, I experienced a lot of depression and several panic episodes. The core group at the church was a wonderful, loving, and very supportive bunch. But the ministry around the church was very high maintenance and stressful. We worked a lot with very low-income and high drug-use neighborhoods.

In 1995, we moved into a new house on property deeded to us by my parents. We started with a modest set of house plans, but money was easy to borrow. And by the time I finished with the house plans, it was twice the size we needed and three times the cost we could afford. All the while I was ignoring the sane and levelheaded suggestions of my wife. I simply allowed my manic tendencies to rule.

We enjoyed living there for about twelve years, but financial pressures we were under caused a lot of stress and curbed some of the joy we might have felt. We did go to a Christian financial advisor in Bentonville, Arkansas. Everything he shared made sense and was so simple. We adopted his advice and begin to make progress. I had enough good sense to know to delegate the financial bookkeeping and spending plan to Marie. If I did not interfere, things went like clockwork. When I interfered, things went quickly awry.

In 2000, I begin Pastoring Union Baptist Church in Harrison, Arkansas. This was Marie's home church. That is where Marie and I first met and where we were married. We had a wonderful and successful ministry, in terms of the breadth and depth of ministry and in terms of growth in numbers. But I began to experience a decline in my physical health as well as my emotional health.

In 2005, I had a heart stint implanted and pacemaker installed. Because of my age and family history, this was not entirely surprising. I also began to experience longer periods of depression and frequent panic attacks. I went to see a psychotherapist on one occasion. It took only the one trip to know he was not going to help me. In 2008 I, was finally diagnosed with a bipolar condition. This came after spending a week on suicide watch in a hospital in Fayetteville, Arkansas. At a later date, I spent a second week in the same hospital.

I remember preaching one Sunday morning while still coming to grips with my diagnosis, making a strange announcement to my congregation. I did know ahead of time I was going to make this announcement. My wife did not know I was going to make this announcement. But I said, "Folks, I am leaving tomorrow for Florida. I will be gone for three or four weeks. It will be a time of recuperation."

What the church did not know was that I had a pastor friend at First Baptist Church, Panama City Beach, who had offered a house where I could stay. Of course, I went alone. I did return in about three weeks, but I brought my problem back with me. Someone had rumored that since I left Marie behind, I must have another lady friend in Florida. That rumor got put down rather quickly once I returned.

My psychiatrist, who is a fine Christian, recommended that I end my pastorate and seek to minister in other ways. So I ended my pastoral ministry in 2008. In took about three months after employing the help of a good attorney to be qualified for Social Security disability. The following year, I tried to be an assistant pastor in a small church, but that did not work for me. I was able to substitute preach from time to time, but even then, I would sometimes develop anxiety.

One of the things that helped me begin to heal was an agreement my buddy, Vic Landis, forced me to sign. He drove over to our apartment one day with a paper that read

> "I will not preach, teach or lead
> in any way a congregation for a
> period of one-year beginning
> Signed Ray Edwards _____
> Vic Landis _____
> (Todays date) until
> (date one year from now)

Vic said he would check on me from time to time and we would take a drive in his Corvette. He called it his "Corvette counseling." He told me we could talk or not talk. We could just look around or just hang out. Previously he had spent an entire year under severe depression and hardly left the house. God had intervened in his situation and had completely lifted the vail of depression. Now he felt compelled to minister to me and, by extension, to Marie. I shall always be grateful to Vic for being such a great friend. I posted that paper on our refrigerator and abided by that commitment for one year. A lot of healing took place that year.

We were members of First Baptist Church, Harrison, Arkansas. Pastor Rob Davis ministered to both Marie and me during that year. Dave Hart, our worship leader, helped lift our hearts and voices in praise every Sunday. It became a trifold balm that promoted emotional and spiritual healing for both Marie and me.

4

WHAT DOES THE BIBLE SAY?

Having been a preacher of the Word of God since I was eighteen years old and having studied the scripture both in a formal and an informal setting, I wanted to know what the Bible had to say about mental illness in general and depression specifically. I saw the roots go back into the words and stories of the Bible. I first looked at some New Testament words that could be translated *depression* in one of its many forms.

There are five Greek words in the New Testament that can help us understand depression as we use the term today. They refer to depression from light to moderate to the most severe cases. They range from sadness to acute mental anguish, loss of hope, despair, and the inability to enjoy life.

1. Skuthropos *(sad, gloomy, or disheartened)*. Jesus said in Matthew 6:16, "Whenever you fast, don't be sad-faced like the hypocrites. For they make their faces unattractive, so their fasting is obvious to people. I assure you: They've got their reward!"

   The Greek word here, *skuthropos*, simple refers to a sad expression. The Pharisees were simply faking a facial appearance to look more spiritual. This would be the extreme of hypocrisy. The word *hypocrisy* means to "act a part" (playacting). This kind of depression is not real.

   The same Greek word is used by Jesus as He spoke to two on their way to Emmaus after the crucifixion in Luke

24:17: "Then He asked them, 'What is this dispute that you're having with each other as you are walking?' And they stopped walking and looked discouraged."

This time it refers to a "sad or discouraged heart" because of what has happened to their Messiah. They were not yet aware of the resurrection. It refers to a genuine sorrow resulting from the loss of one in whom they had put their highest hopes. They simply felt dejected.

2. Stugnasas *(despondent, dejection, discouragement)*. The Bible in Mark 10:21–22 reads,

> Then, looking at him, Jesus loved him and said to him, "You lack one thing: Go, sell all you have and give to the poor, and you will have treasure in heaven. Then come, follow Me." But he was stunned at this demand, and he went away grieving, because he had many possessions.

What is amazing here is that the young man Jesus is talking to was very wealthy and was also a powerful ruler. He was a young man who had most of his life before him. If you read the whole story, you will find that he sought out Jesus to ask Him what he had to do to gain eternal life. He addressed Jesus as "good teacher," but Jesus reminded him that only God is good (of course, Jesus is God). Jesus told him to keep the commandments. He said that he had kept them from his youth. Then Jesus told him he lacked one thing. He must sell his goods, give them to the poor, and come follow the Christ. The scripture says,

> But he was stunned at this demand, and he went away grieving, because he had many possessions.
> (v 22)

The word *grieving* comes from our Greek word that can be translated as "depressed." Our rich young ruler brings it upon himself. He was trusting in his riches rather than trusting in the Lord Jesus Christ.

Are you aware that the suicide rate is highest in the developed nations and there is a rise of suicides every time there is a major downturn in the stock market? If your security is in things, you are an accident waiting to happen.

The greatest death rate among teens is caused by suicide. Young people are depressed today at an alarming rate because the previous generation has for the most part sold them a lie. We have said if you get a good education, you can become anything you want to be and have anything you want to have. We have fed their flesh but starved their spirit. We have taught them *what* but not *why*. We have told them to *aim* for their goals but not helped them learn to *recognize* worthy goals from unworthy goals. We have not helped them learn to make decisions based on *logic* and *reason* but instead focused on *feelings* and *spontaneous mob reaction*.

Many would have the coming generation ignore the lessons of history and live in someone's fantasy bubble. The truth is, there is a day of reckoning coming. We will all stand before a Holy God and give an account.

3. Kataballomenoi *(struck down or lack of pleasure or the capacity to experience it)*. The Bible in 2 Corinthians 4:7–12 says this:

Now we have this treasure in clay jars, so that this extraordinary power may be from God and not from us. We are pressured in every way but not crushed; we are perplexed but not in despair; we are persecuted but not abandoned; we are struck down but not destroyed. We always carry the death of Jesus in our body, so that the life of Jesus may also be revealed in our body. For we who live are always given over to death because of Jesus, so that Jesus' life may also be revealed in our mortal flesh. So death works in us, but life in you.

Paul speaks in the Book of Romans about giving our-selves a living sacrifice. Very few of us can identify with Paul. We talk about being ready to die for Christ, but are we ready to live for Christ? Living for Christ is often much harder than dying.

I often think about those two times when the thought of taking my own life went through my brain. I cannot speak for every person who deals with the thoughts of suicide. It can be a very complicated matter. Tragedies hit people so hard sometimes, it is difficult to distinguish truth from fiction. That is why they need constant godly guidance. But I know that taking my life would have been the coward's way out. God wants a living sacrifice, not a dead one.

This clay vessel Paul refers to in Second Corinthians is our bodies. So my body contains the life and light of God. If it must be broken for the light of Jesus to shine forth, then bring it on. And when death does come, may it be at the hands of the enemy of the cross while I am standing true for the Savior who died for me. I can endure the "thorns" God allows because His Grace is always enough.

4. Exaporeomai *(sorrow, grief, anguish)*. Second Corinthians 1:8–11 teaches us this:

> For we don't want you to be unaware, broth-ers, of our affliction that took place in Asia: we were completely overwhelmed—beyond our strength—so that we even despaired of life. Indeed, we personally had a death sentence within ourselves, so that we would not trust in ourselves but in God who raises the dead. He has delivered us from such a terrible death, and He will deliver us. We have put our hope in Him that He will deliver us again while you join in helping us by your prayers. Then many will give thanks on our behalf for the gift that came to us through the prayers of many.

The phrase "despaired of life" is a Greek word that denotes depression so deep that it indicates that death is imminent. Paul said he despaired of life. Apparently, he was so ill that he would have welcomed death. I remember as a child hearing older folks talk about someone who was at the point of dying. And they would say, "They have the 'death rattles.'" Often the next morning, they would be dead.

As a pastor having to deal with the dying, I have experienced for myself what is referred to as the "death rattles" in those who have a short time to live. I believe Paul had the death rattles. Paul was not only facing death but apparently was experiencing terrible pain. He indeed was experiencing great depression and anguish of soul. Even those around him thought he was going to die. But God brought him back from the very precipice of death. Some scholars believe that his sickness may have resulted in his poor eyesight, which he seems to allude to later in his ministry.

5. Perilupos *(extreme depression, sorrowfulness, feelings of inadequacy, a mood disorder)*. We read in Matthew 26:36–39 this:

Then Jesus came with them to a place called Gethsemane, and He told the disciples, "Sit here while I go over there and pray." Taking along Peter and the two sons of Zebedee, He began to be sorrowful and deeply distressed. Then He said to them, "My soul is swallowed up in sorrow—to the point of death. Remain here and stay awake with Me." Going a little farther, He fell facedown and prayed, "My Father! If it is possible, let this cup pass from Me. Yet not as I will, but as You will."

The phrase "swallowed up in sorrow" contains the Greek word *perilupos*, and it denotes the most extreme form of depression. It would indicate a mood disorder. It is true that whatever we suffer, however great it may be, we can be sure that our Lord Jesus has suffered it as well and in a greater proportion. The scripture tells us that our High Priest, the Lord Jesus, is touched by the feeling of our weaknesses because He was tempted in every possible way that we are, yet He never sinned. We notice this in Hebrews 4:14–16:

Therefore, since we have a great high priest who has passed through the heavens—Jesus the Son of God—let us hold fast to the confession. For we do not have a high priest who is unable to sympathize with our weaknesses, but One who has been tested in every way as we are, yet without sin. Therefore let us approach the throne of grace with boldness, so that we may receive mercy and find grace to help us at the proper time.

The physical passion of Christ began in His suffering and rejection. Of the many aspects of His initial suffering, the one which is of physiological interest is the bloody sweat. Interestingly, the physician, St. Luke, is the only evangelist to mention this occurrence. He says in Luke 22:44, "Being in anguish, He prayed more fervently, and His sweat became like drops of blood falling to the ground."

Every attempt imaginable has been used by modern scholars to explain away the phenomenon of bloody sweat, apparently under the mistaken impression that it simply does not occur. A great deal of effort could be saved by consulting the medical literature. Though very rare, the phenomenon of hematidrosis, or bloody sweat, is well documented. Under great emotional stress, tiny capillaries in the sweat glands can break, thus mixing blood with sweat. This process alone could have produced marked weakness and possible shock.

Oh, my dear friend Jesus came to this earth to bring hope to the hopeless, help to the helpless, light to the darkness, strength to the weak, and healing to the sick. He took upon Himself my gethsemane. It started with the mock trials as they spat upon him and plucked his beard and placed a crown of thorns upon His head. It continued in the garden as He took upon Himself our

- sins
- sorrows
- sufferings
- sicknesses
- depressions
- bipolar conditions
- mental Illnesses of all kinds
- physical infirmities
- weaknesses
- maladies
- curses

and then died in our place and arose from the dead to assure us that God won the victory. And we now share in that victory. Amen!

5

Examples from the Past

Secular History

1. *Charles Hadden Spurgeon.* Charles Hadden Spurgeon knew, by the most painful experience, what deep "depression of spirit" meant, having experienced it countless times. He was one of the greatest British preachers of the nineteenth century. He warned his students,

> Fits of depression come over the most of us. Usually cheerful as we may be, we must at intervals be cast down. The strong are not always vigorous, the wise not always ready, the brave not always courageous, and the joyous not always happy.[1]

Although he said he believed that spiritual darkness of any sort was to be avoided, if at all possible, and not desired.

He never assumed that a Christian suffering depression must necessarily be in sin. In his lectures, Spurgeon noted that some of the great men of God whom he loved and esteemed and who many others consider among the very choicest of God's people wrestled with what he called "fits of depression"—or, in reference to his own times, grave sadness he would call "fainting fits." Far from being judgmental, Spurgeon was understanding and compassionate about this specific battle that so many had to fight.

Spurgeon goes on in his book *Lectures to my Students* to give some of the reason believers fall into "sadness," as he sometimes calls depression. He also provides hope for those so overtaken, adding,

> Is it not first, that they are men? Even under the economy of redemption it is most clear that we are to endure infirmities, otherwise there were no need of the promised Spirit to help us in them. It is of need be that we are sometimes in heaviness. Good men are promised tribulation in this world.[2]

Furthermore, in 2 Corinthians 1:4, God "comforts us in all our affliction, so that we may be able to comfort those who are in any affliction, with the comfort with which we ourselves are comforted by God."

Spurgeon believed that depression might come to some believers for no discernable reason. He did not consider it an illness or a sin but a season in the life of a Christian and an opportunity to demonstrate trust in the God who would one day wipe away every tear.

2. *Winston Churchill.* Winston Churchill is widely regarded as one of the greatest leaders of the twentieth century. He is believed to have suffered from a bipolar disorder. After observing numerous symptoms such as depression, suicidal intention, mania, and a decreased need for sleep, Churchill's doctor, Lord Moran, recounted in his memoir *Winston Churchill: The Struggle for Survival* that he had diagnosed a middle-aged Churchill with bipolar disorder.

    Churchill often referred to his prolonged periods of depression as his "black dog." During these long and intense times of manic depression, Churchill showed little energy, few interests, had little appetite, and had trouble concentrating.[3]

    We learn much about his private behavior from his wife, Clementine. According to her, when his "black dog" had become docile, Churchill exhibited abnormally high levels of energy and restlessness, often beginning to work at 8:00 a.m. and ending work at around 2:00 a.m. Unfortunately, these times of abnormal productivity receded as his "black dog" returned after just a few months of absence. But despite the difficulties brought by his crippling depression, he was able to work through his affliction and fulfill a life of purpose and achievement.[4]

Many believe that Churchill's depression increased his realism and empathy and helped him assess the true dangers that were otherwise overlooked by his colleagues. During World War II, Churchill's heightened skepticism allowed him to realistically evaluate the ever-growing German threat. In World War II, Churchill kept his "black dog on a leash" and kept British spirits high.

He regularly delivered inspiring speeches to Parliament and British citizens. Churchill's foresight and inspirational influences undoubtedly saved the lives of many people and may have even changed the courses of both World War I—or, the Great War, as it was first called—and World War II.

Churchill, in some way, seems to have benefitted from his depressive and manic episodes. With a rare surge of energy, activity, and restlessness, Churchill published forty-three books while upholding his duties as acting prime minister. The pinnacle of Churchill's career as a writer was probably his acceptance of the 1953 Nobel Prize in Literature, which honored several of his published works. Churchill's unbelievable accomplishments are proof that, despite being challenged with a bipolar disorder, individuals today can still achieve great things.

3. *Abraham Lincoln.* Abraham Lincoln was one of our greatest presidents, yet he suffered from depression. It was often called "melancholy" in those days. There was no medical or psychological diagnosis, nor was there any medication that could be prescribed. Perhaps in today's world, he might have been diagnosed

as bipolar, with the most serious and lengthy times being on the depressive side of the scale.

Robert L. Wilson served in the Illinois legislature with Lincoln. Regarding Lincoln's gloominess, Wilson wrote,

> In a conversation with him about that time (1836), he told me that although he appeared to enjoy life rapturously, still he was the victim of terrible melancholy. He sought company, and indulged in fun and hilarity without restraint, or stint as to time. Still when by himself, he told me that he was so overcome with mental depression, that he never dares carry a knife in his pocket. While I was intimately acquainted with him, before the commencement of the practice of the law, he never carried a pocketknife, still he was not a "misanthropic."[5] [Author's explanation: a person who is antisocial and has a distrust of people in general.] He was kind and tender in his treatment to others.

Those around him noticed that Lincoln could go from a happy state to a gloomy one very quickly. Fellow attorney Jonathan Birch said of Lincoln in court,

> His eyes would sparkle with fun, and when he had reached the point in his narrative which invariably evoked the laughter of the crowd, nobody's enjoyment was greater than his. An hour later he might be seen in the same place or in some law office nearby, but, alas, how different! His chair, no longer in the center of the room, would be leaning back against the wall; his feet drawn up and resting on the front rounds so that his knees and chair were about on a level; his hat tipped slightly forward as if to shield his face; his eyes no longer sparkling with fun or merriment, but sad and downcast and his hands

clasped around his knees. There, drawn up within himself as it were, he would sit, the very picture of dejection and gloom. Thus, absorbed have I seen him sit for hours at a time defying the interruption of even his closest friends. No one ever thought of breaking the spell by speech; for by his moody silence and abstraction he had thrown about him a barrier so dense and impenetrable no one dared to break through. It was a strange picture and one I have never forgotten.[6]

Not only did Abraham Lincoln suffer from serious bouts of depression, but he also tried to give advice to others he knew were suffering. Lincoln's depressions—whether they lasted for hours, days, weeks, or months—always came to an end. Knowing this, he could encourage others. It would seem his own experience led him to believe that depression was not a permanent condition.

I personally believe that in the providence of God, Abraham Lincoln was God's man for the nation during the time of its greatest struggles. In the final analysis, it was the supernatural strength of God that gave Lincoln the personal and emotional strength he needed to lead a nation during such a time.

4. *Mary Todd Lincoln.* Scholars may continue to debate the mental and emotional condition of Mary Todd Lincoln, Abraham Lincoln's wife. She was not the most popular of first ladies. At times she would fall into great depression, and at other times, she would spend excessive amounts of money for White House furnishings. Keep in mind she lost two sons and one husband while occupying the White House. That alone would cause depression. After she moved out of Washington, her son Robert had her declared insane and committed her to an asylum. However eccentric she might have been, no historian believes she was deranged. I believe with today's understanding, she probably would have been diagnosed with some sort of a bipolar condition.

Biblical History

1. *King David.* David was troubled and battled deep despair. In many of the psalms, he writes of his anguish, loneliness, fear of the enemy, his heart cry over sin, and the guilt he struggled with because of it. We also see his huge grief in the loss of his sons in 2 Samuel 12:15–23:

> The LORD struck the baby that Uriah's wife had borne to David, and he became ill. David pleaded with God for the boy. He fasted, went home, and spent the night lying on the ground. The elders of his house stood beside him to get him up from the ground, but he was unwilling and would not eat anything with them.
>
> On the seventh day the baby died. But David's servants were afraid to tell him the baby was dead. They said, "Look, while the baby was alive, we spoke to him, and he wouldn't listen to us. So how can we tell him the baby is dead? He may do something desperate."
>
> When David saw that his servants were whispering to each other, he guessed that the baby was dead. So, he asked his servants, "Is the baby dead?"
>
> "He is dead," they replied.
>
> Then David got up from the ground. He washed, anointed himself, changed his clothes, went to the LORD's house, and worshiped. Then he went home and requested something to eat. So, they served him food, and he ate.
>
> His servants asked him, "What did you just do? While the baby was alive, you fasted and wept, but when he died, you got up and ate food."
>
> He answered, "While the baby was alive, I fasted and wept because I thought, 'Who knows? The LORD may be gracious to me and let him

live.' But now that he is dead, why should I fast? Can I bring him back again? I'll go to him, but he will never return to me."

David had committed adultery with Bathsheba, and that had resulted in her becoming pregnant. God had told David through the prophet Nathan that though God forgave him, it meant the sword would not depart from his family. The death of this son was the first result of David's sin. David knew this, but he also recognized the baby that died, he would see again. This is a wonderful Old Testament glimpse of a heavenly revelation. One way to not drown in the depression of today's pitfalls is to delight in tomorrow's promises. The scripture tells us that eyes have never seen, and ears have never heard the glorious, and beautiful things God has prepared for us who really love Him. And one day we will enjoy it all!

The Bible in 2 Samuel 18:33 says, "The king was deeply moved and went up to the gate chamber and wept. As he walked, he cried, "My son Absalom! My son, my son Absalom! If only I had died instead of you, Absalom, my son, my son!"

It is hard to imagine being betrayed by your own son. David's heart was broken. He was sad and despondent beyond description. And yet his love for his son never wavered. Is it any wonder that God would say that David was a man after his heart? David, like Jesus, could love his children even when they betrayed him. David did understand the depth of depression as well as the heights of joy.

In other places, David's honesty with his own weaknesses gives hope to us who struggle today:

- "For my sins have flooded over my head; they are a burden too heavy for me to bear." (Ps. 38:4)
- "Why am I so depressed? Why this turmoil within me? Put your hope in God, for I will still praise Him, my Savior and my God." (Ps. 42:11)

King David: From Delight to Depression to Deliverance
(Poetic paraphrase of Psalm 51)
Raymond F. Edwards

David, a man after God's own heart
Oh, how could it be?
He took another man's wife
And committed adultery

One by one He broke God's laws
To cover up his misdeeds
A crop of wild oats began to grow
For he had sown the seeds

Seeing himself before the Great God
He repented in bitter tears
We see he was different from all other kings
As he ruled for many years

The deepest depression David endured
Started with his great sin
He even suffered physically
And without God he could never win

He asked God to give him the joy he knew
Through the Spirit that lived within
And make his life a witness as before
And see sinners converted again

2. *Jonah.* Jonah was angry and wanted to run away. After God
called Jonah to go to Nineveh to preach to the people, he had a
panic attack. He fled as far away as he could; and after a storm
at sea, being swallowed by a giant fish, and then being saved and
given a second chance, he obeyed. He preached God's message
to the people of Nineveh. Now he was on a spiritual high, having a manic experience.

God's mercy reaches out to all people who turn to Him. But instead of rejoicing, Jonah got angry because a little plant that had grown up to shade his bald head was cut down by a worm. He was waiting outside the city to watch its destruction. He wanted God to destroy it. But God saved the city because they repented at Jonah's preaching. So now we hear pathetic Jonah:

> And now, LORD, please take my life from me, for it is better for me to die than to live.
> Then God asked Jonah, "Is it right for you to be angry about the plant?"
> "Yes," he replied. "It is right. I'm angry enough to die! (Jon. 4:3, 9)

Jonah was more concerned about his reputation and his own comfort than the spiritual welfare of a whole city (Nineveh). When we are ruled by our bipolar or our depression problems, we do become self-absorbed and develop a me-first attitude. This is something we must work through.

3. *Job.* Job suffered through great loss, devastation, and physical illness. This righteous man of God lost literally everything. So great was his suffering and tragedy that even his own wife said in Job 2:9, "Do you still retain your integrity? Curse God and die!"

Though Job maintained his faithfulness to God throughout his life, he still struggled deeply through the trenches of pain, as we read in these verses from the Book of Job:

- "Why was I not stillborn; why didn't I die as I came from the womb?" (3:11)
- "I cannot relax or be still; I have no rest, for trouble comes." (3:26)
- "I am disgusted with my life. I will express my complaint and speak in the bitterness of my soul." (10:1)

- "Terrors are turned loose against me; they chase my dignity away like the wind, and my prosperity has passed by like a cloud. Now my life is poured out before my eyes, and days of suffering have seized me. Night pierces my bones, but my gnawing pains never rest." (30:15–17)

Very few of us suffer as did Job. But we have an advantage that Job did not have. We see his suffering from God's point of view. There are some positive things we do know:

1. God only allows Satan and circumstances to put on us only so much and no more. God is still Sovereign.
2. Right will win in the end.
3. God's grace is always enough.
4. We will understand it all when it is time.
5. Our blessings are always greater than what we give up.

4. *Moses.* Moses was grieved over the sin of his people. In his feelings of anger and betrayal from his own people, Moses, as a leader, was about ready to quit. He came down from his mountaintop experience with God, commandments in hand, only to find the Israelites in complete chaos and sin. He was sad and heartbroken, and he cried out to God on their behalf. You can hear the desperation in his voice:

> So Moses returned to the LORD and said, "Oh, these people have committed a grave sin; they have made a god of gold for themselves.[32] Now if You would only forgive their sin. But if not, please erase me from the book You have written." (Exod. 32:31)

Sometimes it is out of spiritual desperation that we find our spiritual balance and a special strength to fight on. In my own life, it was when I had reached my lowest point, God seemed to do His greatest work in raising me back up.

Let me encourage you by saying

- you are never too low but what God can reach you;
- never too lost but what God can find you;
- never too confused but what God can enlighten you;
- never too heavy but what God can carry you; and
- never too broken but what God can put you back together.

Do I Have a Witness?

5. *Jeremiah.* Jeremiah wrestled with great loneliness, feelings of defeat, and insecurity. Also known as "the weeping prophet," Jeremiah suffered from constant rejection by the people he loved and reached out to. God had called him to preach yet forbade him to marry and have children. He lived alone, he ministered alone, he was poor, ridiculed, and rejected by his people.

During his ministry, he displayed great spiritual faith and strength, yet we also see his honesty as he wrestled with despair and a great sense of failure:

May the day I was born be cursed. May the day my mother bore me never be blessed. May the man be cursed who brought the news to my father, saying, "A male child is born to you," bringing him great joy. Let that man be like the cities the LORD demolished without compassion. Let him hear an outcry in the morning and a war cry at noontime because he didn't kill me in the womb so that my mother might have been my grave, her womb eternally pregnant. Why did I come out of the womb to see only struggle and sorrow, to end my life in shame? (Jer. 20:14–18)

And you thought you had a bad day! Jeremiah was called the *weeping* prophet. But he was also the *reluctant* prophet. He ministered during the declining nation of Judah during its last days. He was the object of scorn and persecution. He presided over Judah's demise as Nebuchadnezzar led his troops into Jerusalem for the first of three assaults that finally destroyed the nation and took them captive for seventy years. But through all this, he faced his discouragement, depression, and what looked like doom with faith in his God. What a lesson for us all.

6. *Saul.* What about King Saul? Israel had clamored for a king. Their reason was not to glorify God but was to be like the other ungodly nations around them. Yet God commissioned Samuel to anoint Saul as Israel's first king.

The scripture says he started out with high poll numbers. He was very attractive. He was head and shoulders taller than most other men. But before long, his true character began to show. The scripture says "an evil spirit from the Lord came upon him." That was another way of saying God allowed him to become insane through demonic activity.

Saul was filled with jealousy, a lust for power, and a spirit of revenge and murder. Saul was God's anointed, but he gave up that right and God replaced him with David. Saul would make a great case study in mental illness brought on by a total disrespect for God.

6

THE ELIJAH SYNDROME

Before we start, we read this in First Kings 18:20–46:

> So Ahab sent for all the children of Israel and gathered the prophets together on Mount Carmel. And Elijah came to all the people, and said, "How long will you falter between two opinions? If the Lord is God, follow Him; but if Baal, follow him." But the people answered him not a word. Then Elijah said to the people, "I alone am left a prophet of the Lord; but Baal's prophets are four hundred and fifty men. Therefore let them give us two bulls; and let them choose one bull for themselves, cut it in pieces, and lay it on the wood, but put no fire under it; and I will prepare the other bull, and lay it on the wood, but put no fire under it. Then you call on the name of your gods, and I will call on the name of the Lord; and the God who answers by fire, He is God."
>
> So, all the people answered and said, "It is well spoken."
>
> Now Elijah said to the prophets of Baal, "Choose one bull for yourselves and prepare it first, for you are many; and call on the name of your god but put no fire under it."

So they took the bull which was given them, and they prepared it, and called on the name of Baal from morning even till noon, saying, "O Baal, hear us!" But there was no voice; no one answered. Then they leaped about the altar which they had made.

And so it was, at noon, that Elijah mocked them and said, "Cry aloud, for he is a god; either he is meditating, or he is busy, or he is on a journey, or perhaps he is sleeping and must be awakened." So they cried aloud, and cut themselves, as was their custom, with knives and lances, until the blood gushed out on them. And when midday was past, they prophesied until the time of the offering of the evening sacrifice. But there was no voice; no one answered, no one paid attention.

Then Elijah said to all the people, "Come near to me." So, all the people came near to him. And he repaired the altar of the Lord that was broken down. And Elijah took twelve stones, according to the number of the tribes of the sons of Jacob, to whom the word of the Lord had come, saying, "Israel shall be your name." Then with the stones he built an altar in the name of the Lord; and he made a trench around the altar large enough to hold two seahs of seed. And he put the wood in order, cut the bull in pieces, and laid it on the wood, and said, "Fill four water pots with water, and pour it on the burnt sacrifice and on the wood." Then he said, "Do it a second time," and they did it a second time; and he said, "Do it a third time," and they did it a third time. So the water ran all around the altar; and he also filled the trench with water.

And it came to pass, at the time of the offering of the evening sacrifice, that Elijah the prophet came near and said, "Lord God of

Abraham, Isaac, and Israel, let it be known this day that You are God in Israel and I am Your servant, and that I have done all these things at Your word. Hear me, O Lord, hear me, that this people may know that You are the Lord God, and that You have turned their hearts back to You again."

Then the fire of the Lord fell and consumed the burnt sacrifice, and the wood and the stones and the dust, and it licked up the water that was in the trench. Now when all the people saw it, they fell on their faces; and they said, "The Lord, He is God! The Lord, He is God!"

And Elijah said to them, "Seize the prophets of Baal! Do not let one of them escape!" So, they seized them; and Elijah brought them down to the Brook Kishon and executed them there.

Then Elijah said to Ahab, "Go up, eat and drink; for there is the sound of abundance of rain." So Ahab went up to eat and drink. And Elijah went up to the top of Carmel; then he bowed down on the ground, and put his face between his knees, and said to his servant, "Go up now, look toward the sea."

So, he went up and looked, and said, "There is nothing." And seven times he said, "Go again."

Then it came to pass the seventh time, that he said, "There is a cloud, as small as a man's hand, rising out of the sea!" So, he said, "Go up, say to Ahab, 'Prepare your chariot, and go down before the rain stops you.'"

Now it happened in the meantime that the sky became black with clouds and wind, and there was a heavy rain. So, Ahab rode away and went to Jezreel. Then the hand of the Lord came upon Elijah; and he girded up his loins and ran ahead of Ahab to the entrance of Jezreel.

We also read this in First Kings 19:1–18:

> And Ahab told Jezebel all that Elijah had done, also how he had executed all the prophets with the sword. Then Jezebel sent a messenger to Elijah, saying, "So let the gods do to me, and more also, if I do not make your life as the life of one of them by tomorrow about this time." And when he saw that, he arose and ran for his life, and went to Beersheba, which belongs to Judah, and left his servant there.
>
> But he himself went a day's journey into the wilderness and came and sat down under a broom tree. And he prayed that he might die, and said, "It is enough! Now, Lord, take my life, for I am no better than my fathers!"
>
> Then as he lay and slept under a broom tree, suddenly an angel touched him, and said to him, "Arise and eat." Then he looked, and there by his head was a cake baked on coals, and a jar of water. So, he ate and drank, and lay down again. And the angel of the Lord came back the second time, and touched him, and said, "Arise and eat, because the journey is too great for you." So he arose and ate and drank; and he went in the strength of that food forty days and forty nights as far as Horeb, the mountain of God.
>
> And there he went into a cave, and spent the night in that place; and behold, the word of the Lord came to him, and He said to him, "What are you doing here, Elijah?"
>
> So he said, "I have been very zealous for the Lord God of hosts; for the children of Israel have forsaken Your covenant, torn down Your altars, and killed Your prophets with the sword. *I alone am left; and they seek to take my life.*"

Then He said, "Go out, and stand on the mountain before the LORD." And behold, the LORD passed by, and a great and strong wind tore into the mountains and broke the rocks in pieces before the LORD, but the LORD was not in the wind; and after the wind an earthquake, but the LORD was not in the earthquake; and after the earthquake a fire, but the LORD was not in the fire; and after the fire a still small voice.

So it was, when Elijah heard it, that he wrapped his face in his mantle and went out and stood in the entrance of the cave. Suddenly a voice came to him, and said, "What are you doing here, Elijah?"

And he said, "I have been very zealous for the LORD God of hosts; because the children of Israel have forsaken Your covenant, torn down Your altars, and killed Your prophets with the sword. *I alone am left; and they seek to take my life.*"

Then the LORD said to him: "Go, *return* on your way to the Wilderness of Damascus; and when you arrive, anoint Hazael as king over Syria. Also you shall anoint Jehu the son of Nimshi as king over Israel. And Elisha the son of Shaphat of Abel Meholah you shall anoint as prophet in your place. It shall be that whoever escapes the sword of Hazael, Jehu will kill; and whoever escapes the sword of Jehu, Elisha will kill. Yet I have reserved seven thousand in Israel, all whose knees have not bowed to Baal, and every mouth that has not kissed him." (Italics mine)

Israel (northern kingdom) was at one of its lowest spiritual points in its corporate history. Ahab and Jezebel were the rulers, and God had cursed the land with a three-year drought. God led Elijah to call a convocation on top of Mount Carmel and have a "spiritual showdown" between Jezebel's prophets of Baal and the God of Israel. The God that answered and consumed the sacrifice by fire would be declared the true God.

Jezebel, of course, never played according to the rules. The people saw God's prophet pray a simple prayer, and a miraculous display of fire from heaven consumed not only the sacrifice but also the barrels of water that Elijah had instructed be poured on the altar.

Israel could have experienced a great revival and probably should have. But what could have and probably should have did not happen. After a threat on his life from the wicked Queen Jezebel, Elijah ran for his life in what seemed to be a complete reversal of his prophetic role. What happened? What caused his panic attack? What caused his depression? What can we learn?

We must understand that we are all susceptible to depression. We may or may not have chronic depression or a bipolar condition as a result of a brain malfunction, but all of us experience situational depression.

James says of Elijah in James 5:17–18,

> Elijah was a man with a nature like ours, and he prayed earnestly that it would not rain; and it did not rain on the land for three years and six months. And he prayed again, and the heaven gave rain, and the earth produced its fruit.

Elijah was a tremendous prophet. In many ways, He was the standout prophet of the entire Old Testament. He became only one of two individuals who passed into heaven without going through the normal route of death. The other person was Enoch, of whom it was said, "He walked with God, and he was not for God took him" (Gen. 5:24).

In another context, we can learn from Elijah what it means to be passionate for God, to be entirely sold out. He is the prime example of the kind of disciple it will take if we ever see America turn back to God.

But even though Elijah was a great prophet, he was not super-human. He was just a man. He was susceptible to the same range of human emotions that we all experience. He seems to have expressed certain characteristics of what we might call today a bipolar episode. That is not to say he would have been diagnosed as bipolar had he been around today. But his experience makes for us a helpful study for those who deal with a bipolar diagnosis.

It is well to note that we may not be bipolar in the classic sense or deal with chronic depression; but we all have moments in our ministries, our work, our responsibilities, or just plain life stresses when we experience symptoms of bipolar or depressive behavior to lesser or greater amounts. Why Elijah makes such a great case study becomes clear as we look a little closer at the Mount Carmel experience. Elijah was emotionally depleted.

Sometimes the most dangerous trigger for depression is right after a spiritual or emotional high or a significant change in one's life. Some of these triggers come in the form of

- retirement,
- children leaving home,
- moving to a smaller place,
- suddenly becoming ill,
- surprising loss of a job, or
- unexpected tragic death.

After I experienced my emotional burnout and had to give up pastoring in 2008, one of my counselors gave me an illustration worth repeating. She explained that all of us who give of ourselves to others do so out of our emotional reservoir. If we do not constantly replenish our reservoir, it will eventually run dry. She told me my emotional reservoir was empty. She was absolutely right. These last few years, my emotional reservoir has been slowly filling again but for different reasons, which God is revealing to me a little at a time.

I like to think of myself as having a bipolar diagnosis rather than simply being bipolar. Since, at this point, God has chosen not to remove this brain dysfunction, I simply trust His grace and power to deal with the symptoms. If you think you might have this condition, you need to seek professional help. You need Christian counseling, but you may also need psychiatric medicine prescribed by a psychiatrist. *Note: Having depression or a bipolar condition is not your choice, but you do have a choice as to how you respond.*

There are several factors that touch upon a depression, bipolar (manic depressive) diagnosis, or other similar emotional/mental problems, including the following:

- They can be *congenital*, which means you are dealing with something you were born with.
- There can be *genetic* factors that were latent until sometime later in life.
- There can be *spiritual* factors, all the way from unforgiveness, unresolved conflict, to actual demonization. My theology does not allow me to believe that a child of God can be totally repossessed by Satan, but they can be controlled and dominated to the point of being incapacitated.
- There can be *physiological* factors that relate to one's overall physical health, weight, lack of exercise, poor diet, breathing toxic air, drinking toxic water, etc.
- There can be *physiological* factors, mental and emotional, such as extreme stress (this often applies to soldiers returning from the battlefield), ministry fatigue, mental fatigue, alcohol or drug abuse, not properly dealing with stress, etc.

Looking for the Signs That Might Lead to Depressive or Emotional Burnout

We must guard against discouragement. Discouragement can be linked to depression, as depression is the first cousin to discouragement What then leads to discouragement?

1. False expectations.
2. Expecting a harvest when there has not been enough sowing. (We do reap what we sow.)

3. Expecting an event to be flawless when there has been no planning.
4. Expecting something different than what God desires. (Remember Paul's "thorn in the flesh.")
5. Expecting there will be no trials or hardships. (Note Jeremiah's complaint.)
6. Expecting something that will highlight your gifts and abilities rather than glorify God. (Study the apostle Peter.)
7. Not having a proper handle on your finances and not understanding why the end of your money comes before the end of the month.
8. Not learning to delegate and then being upset when folks do not seem to help.
9. Expecting every church and people group to react the same to your leadership.
10. Feeling that your problem is always someone else's fault or that you are a victim of bad circumstances.
11. Inability to stay with a job or, if a pastor, moving often.
12. Fatigue and loss of drive.
13. Daydreaming about your next move or next church if you are a pastor (one that will be a perfect fit).
14. Not taking the proper amount of time to relax.
15. Conflict in your family about your responsibilities to them and the time you need to give them.
16. If you are a pastor, dreading every counseling session with someone who is troubled.
17. Not wanting to answer the phone.
18. Unwilling to admit that you might be suffering from depression or a bipolar situation.
19. Sudden weight gain or weight loss.
20. Having trouble focusing.
21. Having trouble making decisions and sticking to them.
22. Strong temptations and being overcome by bad thoughts. (These could be in the form of escape, spending money in a reckless way, sexual misconduct, hurting yourself or someone else, damaging property, etc.)

23. Attempting to hurt yourself or some else.
24. Attempting to engage in bizarre behavior like running away, engaging in bad sexual behavior, or suicide.

Beginning with one symptom, you need to seek the guidance of a strong, wise, and older pastor or leader.

Beginning with twelve, you need to seek professional and/or Christian psychiatric help.

Bipolar simply means that you have wide mood swings from high (manic) to low (depressive). One textbook definition describes bipolar disorder as a major affective disorder in which a person alternates between states of deep depression and extreme elation. This is misleading in that bipolar disorder—also known as manic depression or manic-depressive illness—is much more complicated than just alternating between depression and elation.

The American Psychiatric Association's *Diagnostic and Statistical Manual of Mental Disorders* (commonly known as the DSM-5 because it is in its fifth major edition) indicates that bipolar disorder is characterized by the occurrence of one or more manic or mixed episodes often accompanied by depressive episodes.[1] So even if you are depressed 99 percent of the time, going through just one manic episode qualifies you for a diagnosis of bipolar disorder according to this definition, but that still leaves out a lot of what manic depression really is.

So let us put it in terms everyone can understand. Bipolar disorder is an illness that affects thoughts, feelings, perceptions, and behavior, even how a person feels physically (known clinically as psychosomatic presentations). It is probably caused by electrical and chemical elements in the brain not functioning properly and is usually found in people whose families have a history of one or more mental illnesses. (While we are at it, let us be clear—a mental illness is one that affects the mind, not one that's all *in* the mind.)

Most often, a person with manic-depressive experiences have moods that shift from high to low and back again in varying degrees of severity. The two poles of bipolar disorder are mania and depression. This is the least complicated form of the illness.

Depression might be identified by

- refusing to get out of bed for days on end;
- sleeping much more than usual;
- being tired all the time but unable to sleep;
- having bouts of uncontrollable crying;
- becoming entirely uninterested in things you once enjoyed;
- paying no attention to daily responsibilities;
- feeling hopeless, helpless, or worthless for a sustained period;
- becoming unable to make simple decisions; and
- wanting to die.

Mania might include

- feeling like you can do anything, even something unsafe or illegal;
- needing very little sleep yet never feeling tired;
- dressing flamboyantly, spending money extravagantly, living recklessly;
- having increased sexual desires, perhaps even indulging in risky sexual behaviors;
- experiencing hallucinations or delusions; and
- feeling filled with energy.

Some people think that they are just "over their depression" when they become manic and don't realize this exaggerated state is part of the illness, part of a bipolar disorder. The person who has depression and mania is said to have *bipolar I*.

In addition to bipolar I disorder, the American system of diagnosing this disorder also includes *bipolar II disorder*, which involves symptoms of hypomania instead of full-blown mania.

Hypomania, a less extreme form of a manic episode, could include

- having utter confidence in yourself,
- being able to focus well on projects,
- feeling extra creative or innovative,

- being able to brush off problems that would paralyze you during depression, and
- feeling "on top of the world" but without going over the top.

Hypomania does not include hallucinations or delusions, but a hypomanic person still might exhibit some reckless or inappropriate behavior. A person who has moods of depression and hypomania is said to have bipolar II.[2]

Let us continue now to look at Elijah and get some answers about how to deal with emotional burnout, whether from clinical depression or situational depression. Everyone who has worked for very long at any job or ministry that puts them in constant contact with people has been close to burnout, has experienced burnout, or will be, to some degree in their careers. This does not mean, however, that everyone has clinical depression or is bipolar.

The following are some cautions we need to take note of as we study what I call the "Elijah syndrome." This study has helped me immensely.

1. *Elijah developed what we might call a Messiah complex.*

We read this excerpt from First King 19:10: "So he said, 'I have been very zealous for the LORD God of hosts; for the children of Israel have forsaken Your covenant, torn down Your altars, and killed Your prophets with the sword. *I alone am left; and they seek to take my life* (italics mine)'"

What Elijah was saying was, "I am the only prophet of YAHWEH. If it gets done, I will have to do it!"

Let us be honest. There are times in our positions of leadership we begin to feel that no one can do the job as well as we can. We may not voice it out loud. But if we are not careful, we will begin to micromanage a program and ultimately take on the weight of the responsibility. Our plate continues to fill because we feel nobody else will do it right. Soon we began to think that we are the only one willing to do it. *Wrong!* We are blinded by our success, but we are also headed for a fall. This brings us to our second caution.

2. *Do not take on more responsibility than you can handle because you feel you can do a better job.*

There are no specific signs that Elijah had overloaded himself, but for some reason he seemed not to be aware of the work of other prophets, godly men and women who were serving faithfully the God of Abraham, Isaac, and Jacob. This feeling of carrying the load himself can bring on an emotional and spiritual crisis.

I have learned three very important things about starting ministries in a church I might be pastoring: (1) The need never constitutes the call. There are thousands of needs at any given time, but a single church is not called to start a thousand ministries to meet those needs. We must wait for the voice and direction of God. (2) When God wants to start a ministry, He has someone in mind to lead that ministry. (3) And if I am that someone, God will speak to me, not just through a committee or an influential member. And it will be more than my own personal desire.

The church I pastored prior to my last church, I was overloaded with some tremendous ministries that were life changing for many people. But I was on the verge of burnout. Probably the one thing that kept that from happening was the move to my last church. I was committed and my heart was in all that I was doing, but I was over extended. I had failed to seek the wisdom of God and was failing to properly delegate responsibility.

3. *Trash-talking is really not becoming a prophet of God.*

We read with great delight when Elijah mocks the prophets of Baal and of the Grove, "Maybe your god is taking a journey, or is resting, or asleep" (1 Kings 18:27). One translation notes the Hebrew word used by Elijah mocking the false gods could refer to their "using the toilet." Though God did not reprimand Elijah for his trash-talk, I wonder if it was really called for. It might be all right for football but not necessary for kingdom work.

There is no doubt the whole affair on Mount Carmel was quite a show. The only admission charged was the people's donation of water later that evening. His trash-talk only served to make his panic and run from Jezebel's threat seem even more strange.

The following verses have much to say to New Testament believers concerning the importance of a good dose of humility:

- "Do I take any pleasure in the death of the wicked?" This is the declaration of the Lord God. "Instead, don't I take pleasure when he turns from his ways and lives?" (Ezek. 18:23)
- "Friends, do not avenge yourselves; instead, leave room for His wrath. For it is written: Vengeance belongs to Me; I will repay, says the Lord." (Rom. 12:19)

One of my college professors would often tell us young preacher boys, "If you can preach on the subject of hell without weeping, you should have spent more time praying."

Humility should always be the hallmark of a God called minister. Humility reflects the heart of God. God does not enjoy watching sin take its deadly toll on an individual or a nation. It should cause us to weep. That is why Jeremiah was called the weeping prophet and why Jesus wept over Jerusalem as he returned just prior to His crucifixion.

4. *God used Elijah.*

God was not through with Elijah simply because he had an emotional crash. God is not through with us because we have a temporary emotional crash or some permanent brain/psychological malfunction like depression or a manic-depressive disorder. The call of God is a permanent one. How we serve may change, but who we serve remains the same.

5. *The power of God was on Elijah.*

Often the power of God is demonstrated in a greater degree when the servant of God is at his weakest. Elijah appears to be strong as we see him operate upon Mount Carmel. The truth is, the God for whom Elijah was serving was the one who was strong. Truth be known, Elijah may have been at the point of exhaustion as he called the convocation together that day on Carmel. Only God's power and grace made the whole event a spiritual success.

6. *It seemed that all the forces of hell had broken loose.*

When the power of God is demonstrated, one of two things happens. One is that revival begins to break out and folks begin to get right with almighty God. It looked like this might happen on Mount Carmel after God answered Elijah's prayer by sending down fire from heaven.

The second thing that happens is that God's people become intimidated as the devil unleashes hell's fury. That is what happened after the Carmel demonstration. What could have been Israel's spiritual rebirth became Israel's spiritual abortion. And her response sealed her fate, until 722 BC she was invaded and destroyed by the nation of Assyria. The point is, when God moves, we better be ready to move with Him in the destructive aftermath.

7. *Elijah became afraid—he had a "panic attack."*

Let us be honest, Elijah did not run because he was afraid of Jezebel. He ran because he was totally exhausted. He had a panic attack—an emotional breakdown, an episode of extreme depression. Elijah did not want to see anybody and became very antisocial.

8. *Elijah wanted to die—he became "suicidal."*

Elijah said to the Lord, "I'm no better than our fathers" (1 Kings 19:4). He was saying that he was no better than those who had led Israel into the spiritual mess she was in. So he asked the Lord to simply kill him. He really wanted to die. If he had had a knife, he might well have tried to run it through himself.

I have been asked by a grieving parent whose son took his own life, "Will he go to heaven?" My answer is, "If he was saved, born again, of course he will go to heaven. In fact, he is already there."

Is it wrong to take your life? Of course it is. But it is not the unpardonable sin. One of my best friends, a great man of God, one who helped ordain me to the ministry, ended his life with his own gun. I asked the minister who preached his funeral how he handled it. He said he told those attending his service the important thing was not how he died but how he lived.

I have been asked the question as to how a Christian can even contemplate suicide? I will attempt to answer that question. We read this in the Word:

> If any of you lacks wisdom, you should ask God, who gives generously to all without finding fault, and it will be given to you. But when you ask, you must believe and not doubt, because the one who doubts is like a wave of the sea, blown and tossed by the wind. That person should not expect to receive anything from the Lord. Such a person is double-minded and unstable in all they do. (Jam. 1:5–8, NIV)

Of being double-minded, the New Century Version says, "Thinking two different things at the same time, and they cannot decide about anything they do."

If you have ever experienced some severe form of rash, the doctor may have treated it and instructed you not to scratch it no matter how much it may itch. Scratching it would spread it, prolong the healing, and risk a secondary infection. The itch was almost unbearable. One side of your brain was telling you to scratch the dickens out of it. And many times, you would start. The other side of your brain would tell you it would not be worth the risk and to just hold on. It was a mental battle that went on for several days, and were it not for the support of your wife and others, you might have given in to the urge to scratch.

Battles are won or lost in the mind. Know that the human mind is more than the brain. The human brain is an organ like your liver, lungs, or pancreas. Your mind is part of your soul (life), part of the breath of God that gives you self-awareness. You may be having brain dysfunction, but your mind can still function with the help of the creator.

Keep before you what Paul said in Romans 12:2: "Do not conform to the pattern of this world but be transformed by the renewing of your mind. Then you will be able to test and approve what God's will is—his good, pleasing and perfect will" (NIV).

The New Century Version says, "Be changed from within by a new way of thinking."

Twice I was under suicide watch for about a week each time. Both times I was driving a car when the thought of hurting myself began to plague my mind. One side of my brain was saying go for that tree in the field at full speed. I began to turn the wheel in that direction. The other side of my brain asked, "*How fast would you have to go?*" The other side of my brain kicked in and asked, "*Might you be just a vegetable? What about your family? What about the witness I would leave behind What about your wife?*" I turned the wheel back toward the roadway.

The second time it happened, I called my psychiatrist. The nurse answered, and after telling her my situation, she told me to get to the nearest emergency center. I called my wife, and she stayed on the phone with me until I met her at the hospital.

I am a Christian, but I was experiencing a brain malfunction. When you have a heart attack, you are experiencing a heart malfunction. If you are hypoglycemic or hyperglycemic, you are experiencing a pancreatic malfunction. The brain responds to certain chemical enzymes, electric impulses, and food and oxygen from the blood, not unlike any other body organ. Again, remember, your mind and your brain are not the same thing.

What can aid our healing or at least help us live with our diagnosis, whether a brain malfunction or a malfunction of any other body organ, is to know how to renew our mind and to have a support system in place. More will be said about this later in the book.

Often because of the nature of our work as ministers of the Gospel, we feel we must be "spiritual" enough not to have to seek professional help for depression or similar psychological problems.

This, of course, is far from the truth and often makes our situation worse. It certainly did in my case.

Below is an article written by Toni Ridgaway, taken from the September 11, 2010, issue of USA Today:

> What kind of personal pain would cause a 42-year-old pastor to abandon his family, his calling and even life itself? Members of a Baptist church here are asking that question after their pastor committed suicide in his parked car in September.
>
> Those who counsel pastors say Christian culture, especially Southern evangelicalism, creates the perfect environment for depression. Pastors suffer in silence, unwilling or unable to seek help or even talk about it. Sometimes they leave the ministry. Occasionally the result is the unthinkable.
>
> Experts say clergy suicide is a rare outcome to a common problem. But Baptists in the Carolinas are soul-searching after a spate of suicides and suicide attempts by pastors. In addition to the September suicide of David Treadway, two others in North Carolina attempted suicide, and three in South Carolina succeeded, all in the last four years.
>
> Being a pastor—a high-profile, high-stress job with nearly impossible expectations for success—can send one down the road to depression, according to pastoral counselors. "We set the bar so high that most pastors can't achieve that," said H.B. London, vice president for pastoral ministries at Focus on the Family, based in Colorado Springs, Colo. "And because most pastors are people-pleasers, they get frustrated and feel they can't live up to that." When pastors fail to live up to demands imposed by themselves or others

they often "turn their frustration back on themselves," leading to self-doubt and to feelings of failure and hopelessness, said Fred Smoot, executive director of Emory Clergy Care in Duluth, Georgia.

Most counselors and psychologists interviewed for this article agreed depression among clergy is at least as prevalent as in the general population. As many as 12% of men and 26% of women will experience major depression during their lifetime, according to the American Medical Association. "The likelihood is that one out of every four pastors are depressed," said Matthew Stanford, a professor of psychology and neuroscience at Baylor University in Waco, Texas. But anxiety and depression in the pulpit are "markedly higher" in the last five years, said Smoot. "The current economic crisis has caused many of our pastors to go into depression." Besides the recession's strain on church budgets, depressed pastors increasingly report frustration over their congregations' resistance to cultural change.

Nearly two out of three depressed people don't seek treatment, according to studies by the Depression and Bipolar Support Alliance. Counselors say even fewer depressed ministers get treated because of career fears, social stigma and spiritual taboo. "Clergy do not talk about it because it violates their understanding of their faith," said Scoggin. "They believe they are not supposed to have those kinds of thoughts." Stanford, who studies how the Christian community deals with mental illness, said depression in Christian culture carries "a double stigmatization." Society still places a stigma on mental illness, but Christians make it worse, he said, by "over-spiritualizing" depression and other disorders—dismissing them as a lack of faith or a sign of weakness. Polite Southern culture adds its own taboo against "talking about something as personal as your mental health," noted Scoggin. The result is a culture of avoidance. "You can't talk about it before it happens, and you can't talk about it after it happens," said Monty Hale, director of pastoral ministries for the South Carolina Baptist Convention.

For pastors, treatment can come at a high price. In some settings, however, it is becoming more acceptable for clergy to get treatment. "Depression is part of the human condition," added Scoggin. "Some people simply find ways to gracefully live with it. Like other chronic illnesses, you may not get over it."

Experts at Gordon-Conwell Theological Seminary suggest that pastors can help prevent depression by engaging in intentional replenishment weekly or monthly, confiding in their spouse and seeking spiritual direction with another pastor who ministers to them. They should also establish boundaries and set realistic expectations. "Jesus did not heal everyone, even though it was within His power to do so. No one is capable of successfully ministering to every person in need," said Drs. Sidney Bradley and Kelly Boyce with GCTS. "Pastors can also normalize the problem of depression by teaching about it. This can help people understand it, and dispel the idea that Christians are immune from depression. Research has shown that when therapy is combined with medication, there is a 90 percent successful treatment rate. Depression is very, very treatable."[3]

9.   *God renewed his mind and body—God provided him food, water, and rest.*

God gave Elijah some Divine medicine from heaven's pharmacy. It was so powerful, he went the next forty days in the strength of it. Wow!

There is nothing wrong with good nourishment, plenty of water, and the right amount of rest. In fact, God expects us to take care of His temple or sanctuary, as the Word teaches us:

> Don't you know that your body is a sanctuary of
> the Holy Spirit who is in you, whom you have
> from God? You are not your own, for you were
> bought at a price. Therefore, glorify God in your
> body. (1 Cor. 6:19–20)

Neither is there anything wrong with taking proper food supplements based on what our body needs and medicine from a trusted doctor that can help control the symptoms of our mental, emotional, or psychological disorder. There is a connection between mental health and physical health. They go hand in hand. We know it is important to keep physically fit. We need to exercise, watch what we eat, and keep our weight under control.

10.   *Elijah had a divine encounter.*

He spilled his guts to God. He was not afraid to be open and honest with God about how he really felt. God knows anyway. When we pray, we need to talk to God as a friend and just tell Him exactly how we feel.

He learned to listen to the voice of God. He did not listen to the noise. He did not make decisions based on emotions. He did not choose his next move in the heat of the moment. He waited until he was sure he had heard the voice of God. After his burnout, he anointed two kings and anointed and trained his successor, Elisha.

No, God was not through with him. Your greatest work may be after you begin to deal with a mental or emotional challenge.

First Steps to Take Once You Know There Is a Problem

1. *Admit your problem.* (Elijah at the brook was very open with God.) You need to spend time with Christ, your Bible, your mate, friends you can trust, and a genuine Christian counselor to determine the source of your problem. Is it disobedience to God, situational depression, genetic in origin, physiological, something else, or some combination of all the above?
2. *Get in touch with your emotions.* (Again, Elijah cried out to his God.) It is okay to cry out to God. To express your feelings openly to those you can trust.
3. *Rest.* (Elijah slept, and an angel of the Lord fed him and gave him water to drink.) Sometimes the most spiritual thing you can do is take a nap

    I heard Vance Havner during one of his speaking engagements at Southwest Baptist College say, "We must come apart and rest or we will just plain come apart." And the Bible also says this: "And he said unto them, 'Come ye yourselves apart into a desert place, and rest a while': for there were many coming and going, and they had no leisure so much as to eat" (Mark 6:31).
4. *Find you a cave.* (Note that Elijah was in a cave.) Get alone with God.
5. *Listen for the voice of God.* (Note how Elijah heard.) Take the following precautionary steps before you do:

    - It may not be in a lot of noise (wind).
    - It may not come with a lot of feeling (earthquake).
    - It may not be in the heat of religious fervor (fire).
    - Sometimes the voice comes directly from the Holy Spirit (still, small voice).
    - Sometimes that voice comes from the Word of God.
    - Sometimes it comes from a pastor or another Christian leader you can trust.

- Often it comes from your mate.
- Sometimes it comes from a counselor. (Make sure it is Christian counseling, not just a Christian that counsels.) This has been so important for me, Dr. Donnie Holden, my personal psychiatrist, counsels from a biblical worldview.

6. *Be willing to do what God tells you.* (God had more tasks for Elijah to do.) He anointed two future kings and the prophet Elisha to replace himself.

7. *Learn to say no and to say no without feeling guilty.* The following is a devotional by Ron Hutchcraft that makes the point about saying *no*:

> If you want to get into Manhattan from New Jersey, you have several choices. You can take a long bridge, one of two long tunnels, a ferry trip, or a long un-recommended swim. The Hudson River is very wide when it reaches Manhattan, but it's not very powerful. If you could see the Hudson River near its headwaters in upstate New York, man, it's roaring along with a strong current. Upstate its banks are confined, and the force is greater. By the time it reaches Manhattan, it's not so powerful. The Hudson's so spread out that its power seems kind of weak by comparison. I know people like that.
>
> Just like the Hudson River, we tend to get spread over too many commitments, don't you think? And sometimes we don't have much power in any of them. We tend to accumulate commitments instead of making choices. We add new arenas without removing any old ones. Homework competes with extracurricular commitments, household responsibilities, youth meetings, friends. A businessperson says "yes" until his or her résumé looks impressive,

but their contributions in each area are kind of insignificant. An overcommitted woman needs a valet just to manage all her hats: wife, mother, committee worker, volunteer, career person, creator, entertainer. By taking on more than we can possibly do well, we live in a direct violation of God's command to *"make it your ambition to lead a quiet life" (1 Thessalonians 4:11)*.

All of us battle those pressures. And the difference we make in each area is always equal to the number of times we say *no*. It was a word Jesus knew how to say no.[4] (Emphasis mine)

Luke 4:40, 42 *also teaches us,*

When the sun was setting, the people brought to Jesus all who had various kinds of sickness, and… He healed them… At daybreak Jesus went out to a solitary place. The people were looking for him and they tried to keep him from leaving them.

But he said, "I must preach the good news of the kingdom of God to the other towns also, because that is why I was sent."

There were always more demands on His time than He could possible do in His earthly body. If Jesus Christ had to decide between the good and the necessary, then we must learn to make those decisions as well. That becomes very difficult for someone with a bipolar condition. Please believe me.

As I have said before, the need does not constitute the call. You can only be your best at a minimum number of things. God has someone else to take up the slack. Saying no is a mark of maturity and an opportunity to minister another day; it is not a cop-out or a shirking of responsibility. Never let Satan's accusations get to you at this point.

8. *Never feel guilty about experiencing the symptoms of your condition.*

9. *Stay on your medication.* (God gave Elijah some very powerful medicine. In fact, he went for forty days in the strength of that medicine.) Medicine is not from the devil, and it is not compromising your faith to take it for mental problems. God has placed within the trees and plants of our world, likely, the cure for most of our problems when we finally get smart enough to know how to use them. Accept the fact that most likely you will need to change some medications every three or four years.

10. *Learn to be comfortable* with the fact that many people including, Christians, will not understand or even sympathize with your condition. Do not let others place you under a cloud of guilt.

11. *Develop a support network.* Gather a small group of true friends that love you, will pray for you and hold you accountable. Have some, like your Psychiatrist, your counselor or therapist, and a small support group with a solid leader that you can meet with weekly. If your problem is not as great, your support group would not include all the above. (Elijah had his support group back soon)

12. *You need at least one close friend* with whom you can be totally open and honest and share your deepest fears and thoughts without concern of your trust being betrayed. (I think for Elijah, this must have been his successor, Elisha.)

13. *You need to meet with a small prayer group* that has some knowledge of your struggle.

14. *You need a pastor who will pray and minister to you.* My pastor, Rob Davis has been a great aid in my emotional and psychological healing, as well as that of my wife, Marie.

15. *Your marriage partner needs to be on the same page with you.* You must work and pray to travel this road together. Marie has been my faithful caregiver. I hope she will write a booklet about her experiences that might prove helpful to those spouses who must deal daily with a life partner who has a chronic mental or emotional problem such as depression, bipolar, or other chronic condition.

Our problem is not depression or *having* a burnout. We may not have a choice. Our challenge is *how to respond*. In that, we do have a choice.

I remember a godly friend coming up to me after a meeting where I had shared my bipolar diagnosis. He laid his hands on me and said, "Brother Ray, I believe God is going to make the next portion of your ministry greater than what has gone before." I took that as a word from the Lord. God has already started confirming that in several ways.

Remember, God is not through with you. Like Paul, you may have to learn to live with the thorn, but the grace of God is sufficient.

Part II

My Story and Living with a Bipolar Diagnosis

7

EXPERIENCING THE LIVING GOD

Isaiah was depressed over the death of his cousin, Uzziah, the king. Sometimes depression is a sign we need to get back in touch with God. I am talking about an intimate experience with God. Notice what happened to Isaiah in Isaiah 6:1–8:

> In the year that King Uzziah died, I saw the Lord seated on a high and lofty throne, and His robe filled the temple. Seraphim were standing above Him; each one had six wings: with two he covered his face, with two he covered his feet, and with two he flew. And one called to another:
>
> Holy, holy, holy is the LORD of Hosts; His glory fills the whole earth.
>
> The foundations of the doorways shook at the sound of their voices, and the temple was filled with smoke.
>
> Then I said:
>
> Woe is me for I am ruined because I am a man of unclean lips and live among a people of unclean lips, and because my eyes have seen the King, the LORD of Hosts.
>
> Then one of the seraphim flew to me, and in his hand was a glowing coal that he had taken

from the altar with tongs. He touched my mouth
with it and said:

Now that this has touched your lips, your
wickedness is removed and your sin is atoned for.

Then I heard the voice of the Lord saying:
Who should I send? Who will go for Us?
I said:
Here I am. Send me.

Isaiah needed to have an intimate experience with God. He
needed to see God's glory. In some of the Jewish writings, this glory
is called the "shekinah," or God's living manifestation. Look at the
conversation Jesus had with Philip below:

"Lord," said Philip, "show us the Father, and
that's enough for us."

Jesus said to him, "Have I been among you all
this time without your knowing Me, Philip? The
one who has seen Me has seen the Father. How
can you say, 'Show us the Father'?" (John 14:8–9)

Look at the experience of Moses:

Moses said to the LORD, "Look, You have told
me, 'Lead this people up,' but You have not let
me know whom You will send with me. You said,
'I know you by name, and you have also found
favor in My sight.' Now if I have indeed found
favor in Your sight, please teach me Your ways,
and I will know You and find favor in Your sight.
Now consider that this nation is Your people."

Then He replied, "My presence will go with
you, and I will give you rest."

"If Your presence does not go," Moses
responded to Him, "don't make us go up from
here. How will it be known that I and Your peo-

ple have found favor in Your sight unless You go with us? I and Your people will be distinguished by this from all the other people on the face of the earth."

The LORD answered Moses, "I will do this very thing you have asked, for you have found favor in My sight, and I know you by name."

Then Moses said, "Please, let me see Your glory."

He said, "I will cause all My goodness to pass in front of you, and I will proclaim the name Yahweh before you. I will be gracious to whom I will be gracious, and I will have compassion on whom I will have compassion." But He answered, "You cannot see My face, for no one can see Me and live." The LORD said, "Here is a place near Me. You are to stand on the rock, and when My glory passes by, I will put you in the crevice of the rock and cover you with My hand until I have passed by. Then I will take My hand away, and you will see My back, but My face will not be seen." (Exod. 33:12–23)

Moses was at a point in leading the Israelites where he was tired, depressed, and discouraged. He needed to experience God in a fresh way. Ne needed to see the glory of God to move on. Many scholars believe that Moses saw a *Christophany*, or a Pre-New Testament (pre-incarnate) appearance of Jesus Christ.

Often our need is to see the glory (shekinah) of God to have a personal experience with God. This shekinah would have been the pillar of fire that led the children of Israel across the wilderness toward the Promised Land.

This is what happened to Isaiah. That which brought Isaiah to this place and desire was a bad situation, a tragedy. Isaiah's friend and cousin had died.

Often midst sorrow, tragedy, and hard times, when we have feelings of fatigue, we desire to touch God, to see Him, to experience Him in a fresh way, and that is good. I am not suggesting that we will see God as Isaiah did, but we can experience Him in a personal, intimate, fresh, and powerful way. We can see Him with a new set of spiritual eyes, sense His presence with a renewed heart, and hear Him with a new pair of anointed ears.

Sometimes God must put us against the wall or allow us to be against the wall to get our attention. Sometimes we are against the wall of suffering, or sorrow, or maybe sickness. First, there must be a spiritual hunger if we are to see God. "Blessed are they that hunger and thirst after righteousness for they shall be filled," Matthew 5:6 says. "Blessed are the pure in heart for they shall see God," we read further in Matthew 5:8. ("Pure in heart" means one must have the right motives, right focus, and right desire.)

Then you need to go to the right place to see God. Isaiah knew where to go, the place of His presence. This was Solomon's temple where God's glory, His presence, moved in after the dedication. You and I must go to the place of His presence, to our own altars or amidst God's people—a place of His manifest presence. We understand God's *sovereign presence*. (He is everywhere at the same time.) We know about His *indwelling presence*. (He lives within every believer.) But we often forget how important His *manifest presence* is. That is where He demonstrates Himself to be real and personal. His manifest presence is what each of us needs to keep us encouraged and to keep our heart on spiritual things.

So like Isaiah, Philip, and Moses—we need to see God, to experience Him. But how do we know when we have seen Him?

1.   *First, we know we have seen Him when we have seen the Lord's majesty (vv 1–4).*

The world today wants to make God like a man. They want to take God down from heaven and make Him one of us. They serve a god they can control.

Recently I heard a dialogue between Senator Bernie Sanders and a man named Vought, who was the deputy director of the Office of Management and Budget for the US government. In the exchange, Sanders refers to a comment that was written by Vought in a publication called *Resurgent*.[1]

SANDERS. Let me get to this issue that has bothered me and bothered many other people. And that is in the piece that I referred to that you wrote for the publication called Resurgent. You wrote, "Muslims do not simply have a deficient theology. They do not know God because they have rejected Jesus Christ, His Son, and they stand condemned." Do you believe that that statement is Islamophobic?

VOUGHT. Absolutely not, Senator. I'm a Christian, and I believe in a Christian set of principles based on my faith. That post, as I stated in the questionnaire to this committee, was to defend my alma mater, Wheaton College, a Christian school that has a statement of faith that includes the centrality of Jesus Christ for salvation, and—

SANDERS. I apologize. Forgive me, we just don't have a lot of time. Do you believe people in the Muslim religion stand condemned? Is that your view?

VOUGHT. Again, Senator, I'm a Christian, and I wrote that piece in accordance with the statement of faith at Wheaton College.

SANDERS. I understand that. I don't know how many Muslims there are in America. Maybe a couple million. Are you suggesting that all those people stand condemned? What about Jews? Do they stand condemned too?

VOUGHT. Senator, I'm a Christian.

SANDERS, shouting. I understand you are a Christian, but this country is made of people who are not just—I understand that Christianity is the majority religion, but there are other people of different religions in this country and around the world. In your judgment, do you think that people who are not Christians are going to be condemned?

VOUGHT. Thank you for probing on that question. As a Christian, I believe that all individuals are made in the image of God and are worthy of dignity and respect regardless of their religious beliefs. I believe that as a Christian that's how I should treat all individuals—

SANDERS. You think your statement that you put into that publication, they do not know God because they rejected Jesus Christ, His Son, and they stand condemned, do you think that's respectful of other religions?

VOUGHT. Senator, I wrote a post based on being a—

SANDERS. I would simply say, Mr. Chairman, that this nominee is really not someone who this country is supposed to be about.

It seems to this author that Bernie Sanders needs to read the Constitution of the United States. He would find there our Founding Fathers very wisely included language that would prohibit imposing a religious test for public office. I fear that Senator Sanders's knowledge of the Bible is no better than his knowledge of the constitution, if you can glean anything from his discussion with Mr. Vought.

Our Founding Fathers were not trying to exclude God from public or political life. They simply did not want to favor one church over another. It was not so much freedom *from* religion they sought as freedom *of* religion. Most, whether they had a personal relationship with Jesus Christ or not, stood in reverence for the person and nature of God. The God of the Bible was looked upon with respect. Within my lifetime, our nation has, by and large, lost that respect.

We must see God today as being in charge, as one who is still in control. Isaiah 6:1–4 says,

> In the year that King Uzziah died, *I saw the Lord seated on a high and lofty throne,* and His robe

filled the temple. Seraphim were standing above Him; each one had six wings: with two he covered his face, with two he covered his feet, and with two he flew. And one called to another:

Holy, holy, holy is the LORD *of Hosts; His glory fills the whole earth.*

The foundations of the doorways shook at the sound of their voices, and the temple was filled with smoke. (Italics mine)

We must see God as high—He is on the Throne. Exodus 15:18 says, "The LORD will reign forever and ever!" However, this does not mean high like the *sky*; it means high in *authority*!

The Lord is the Court of Last Appeals. There is *no one higher*, no one else to appeal to! It is not our educational system, the latest politically correct pronouncement, the current worldview, Hollywood fad, or even the latest scientific breakthrough.

We must see God as Holy. Imagine if you could go up to heaven and listen to what the angels have to say! Would you want to know what the angels would be saying to one another? Isaiah heard what the angel's said. Listen! "Holy, Holy, Holy is the Lord God of hosts, the whole earth is full of His glory!"

Yes, God is mercy, He is kindness, He is goodness, and He is love! Yet above all that God is, one attribute is the foundation of all the rest—*His holiness*!

First John 1:5 says, "Now this is the message we have heard from Him and declare to you: God is light, and there is absolutely no darkness in Him."

For God to be holy means

- to be distinct, separate, in a class by oneself;
- to be morally pure; and
- to be perfect in relation to every aspect of His nature and character.

We must see God as here. His glory fills the whole earth. The word *glory* here means to put something on open display. In other words, God is openly displayed in all His creation that surrounds us.

Is it any wonder the angels cried out *"Holy, holy, holy"*? The first angel must have thought, *"What is God's supreme characteristic? Oh yes, holy!"* The second angel must have thought, *"How can I top that? I can't, for holiness is God's highest characteristic,"* so he shouted louder, *"Holy!"* The third angel thought, *"How can I top that? No way."* So, he shouted even louder, *"Holy!"*

Psalms 19:1 says, "The heavens declare the glory of God, and the sky proclaims the work of His hands."

Several years ago, I was pastor of a church in Albany, Oregon. As I recall, a little eight-year-old girl had accepted Christ as her Savior. Her mother was to pick her up after church. For some reason, the mother was late. So our family waited with the girl until her mother arrived.

I remember it being a beautiful spring day, and the flowers in the bed along one side of the sanctuary were in full bloom. The girl was squatted down just looking at the flower bed. I walked up to where she was and inquired as to exactly what she was doing. Her answer surprised but blessed me. She said, "Pastor, I was watching a honeybee go from one flower to another. You know, before I was saved, I just wanted to squash all the bees, but now I can see how beautiful they are."

God is perfectly displayed in Jesus Christ. Notice the following Scripture passages:

- "Long ago God spoke to the fathers by the prophets at different times and in different ways. In these last days, He has spoken to us by His Son. God has appointed Him heir of all things and made the universe through Him." (Heb. 1:1–2)
- The Word became flesh and took up residence among us. We observed His glory, the glory as the One and Only Son from the Father, full of grace and truth. (John 1:14)

His very name is Emmanuel—God with us!

2. *Next, We know we have experienced God when we see the Lord's mercy (vv 5–7).*

> Then I said:
>> Woe is me for I am ruined because I am a man of unclean lips and live among a people of unclean lips, and because my eyes have seen the King, the LORD of Hosts.
>> Then one of the seraphim flew to me, and in his hand was a glowing coal that he had taken from the altar with tongs. He touched my mouth with it and said:
>> Now that this has touched your lips, your wickedness is removed and your sin is atoned for. (Isa. 6:5–7)

We see His mercy when we admit our destiny. Isaiah 6:5 says, "Woe is me, for I am undone" (KJV). His mercy comes to us as we admit our need, our condition. Literally he says, "I am on my way to destruction, I am perishing." To undo a building, you destroy it. The destiny of man outside of Christ is an eternity in hell!

If you have ever watched a building being wired for demolition, then you would hear a final warning to clear the area. A time would be set for so many minutes before the explosion would bring the building down. One final sweep of the area would be made, the countdown would start, and then *boom*! A cloud of dust signifies just that—total destruction. That is an illustration of our future without Christ.

We see His mercy when we acknowledge our depravity. This is symbolized as we read further in Isaiah 6:5: "I am a man of unclean lips, and I dwell in the midst of a people of unclean lips: for mine eyes have seen the King, the LORD of hosts" (KJV).

We are completely unable to please God! We are undone! We are useless, powerless, helpless, but *not hopeless*!

We see His mercy when we accept our deliverance. "Thine iniquity is taken away, and thy sin is purged" (KJV), we read in the final verse of Isaiah 6.

This altar is the altar of burnt offering, which was kindled by the Lord, and burned continually day and night. Our only hope for deliverance is in the blood of Jesus Christ. The coal was put on Isaiah's lips, and he was not consumed. The reason is because *the Sacrifice was already consumed.* The price had already been paid.

Hebrews 10:4 says, "For it is impossible for the blood of bulls and goats to take away sins." First John 1:7 builds on this by saying, "But if we walk in the light as He Himself is in the light, we have fellowship with one another, and the blood of Jesus His Son cleanses us from all sin."

3.   *Thirdly, we know we have experienced God when we respond to His mission (v 8).*

Isaiah surrendered to His Call. "Then said I, here am I; send me," he says in Isaiah 6:8. Isaiah sees God and realizes his own condition, and he says, "Here am I, Lord, you saw me—I'm a man of unclean lips, I am perishing. Oh God, are you sure you have the right one?" And at the same time, he says, "Here am I, Lord, look at my hands—they are clean, and my mouth is pure, mine iniquity is taken away and my sin purged. Send me!"

You have not experienced God until you say "Send me!"

Finally, what happens after we see God?

- We see ourselves.
- We see others.
- We see our calling.
- We see the direction we should go.

I invite you today to experience God in a deeper way than you have before or deeper than you have in a long time. This is the basis for the greatest and most lasting emotional and mental therapy you can experience.

8

THE HEALING OF RIGHT RELATIONSHIPS

Early in my Christian life, I learned the importance of forgiveness. I knew from the Bible the importance of asking for forgiveness and forgiving others. But it took a lot of living before I understood how easy it was to be deceived by our feelings and our own heart and mind, if not led by the Holy Spirit and the Word of God. I have seen how easy it is to be blinded by Satan's lies as he Covers over the truth. So, many years ago, I began praying this as part of my daily prayer:

> Search me, O God, and know my heart: try me,
> and know my thoughts:
> > And see if there be any wicked way in me,
> and lead me in the way everlasting. (Ps. 139:23–24, KJV)

After I began my post-emotional burnout with the "bipolar thorn" that God, in His grace and providence, has allowed me to have, there have been two important experiences with forgiveness. Both have brought a great deal of inner peace and healing. I believe God was answering the prayer of Psalm 139:23–24.

There was one experience where I was confronted with some events that had happened while my son was still at home. I had wronged him but had never ask his forgiveness. I knew I had to write him a letter and make things right. I did so. I sought his forgiveness.

The second experience happened as a result of a session with one of my godly counselors. This time, it had to do with giving forgiveness. He gave me an assignment to go home and take a sheet of paper. On that paper I was to write the name of any person toward whom I might have the slightest amount of anger or bitterness.

Beside their name, I was to write down what they might have said or done that made me feel negative toward them. He told me this might have happened years ago. The person might even be dead. They probably do not even know they offended me. This person might be my spouse or one of my children and the offense could have been decades ago.

Once on that list, which may include myself or even the Lord (yes, I might be angry at God), pray over the list one name at a time. Pronounce "forgiven," "no more anger," and "no more grudges." Say to God in each case, "I give up my assumed right to be angry."

I did what the counselor told me to do. Then he had instructed me to light a match to it, and put it in my grill and watch it burn and rejoice in the Lord that I was now free from any unforgiveness. I can tell you, it was like a two-ton weight had been lifted off my shoulders.

In this chapter, I have an assignment for you. You can make a copy of this page or just use the following as a guide. I believe it will prove a blessing for any believer whether you have a mental or emotional problem or not.

The first assignment is asking forgiveness. If you have never really asked God's forgiveness, now is the right time. What you need to ask is forgiveness that you have not trusted and believed on His Son, Jesus Christ, to be your Lord and Savior and forgive you for all the past. And then receive Him into your life as a personal friend and one you promise to be obedient to. Now you are ready to be more specific in your healing of right relationships.

Asking for Forgiveness

If we confess our sins, He is faithful and just
to forgive us our sins and to cleanse us from all
unrighteousness. (1 John 1:9, KJV)

Lord, please forgive me for wrong feelings, attitudes, words, and actions (name them) I have had regarding (name the person especially the Lord).

Be specific. Write the person/action/words/thoughts below.

_____

_____

_____

_____

_____

_____

I confess I have no right to hold bitterness in my heart or to be offensive to anyone even myself. Thank you for your forgiveness. I receive it by faith. Help me from this point on to be obedient to you in this matter.

Therefore if you bring your gift to the altar, and
there remember that your brother has something against you, leave your gift there before
the altar, and go your way. First be reconciled to
your brother, and then come and offer your gift.
(Matt. 5:23–24, KJV)

Explanation: This is how I want you to conduct yourself in these matters. If you enter your place of worship and about to make an offering, you suddenly remember a grudge a friend has against you, abandon your offering, leave immediately, go to this friend, and make things right. Then and only then, come back and work things out with God.

Note: If your feelings, attitudes, words, or actions are known by these people (name individuals)-

_____

_____

_____

_____

then pray, "Help me go to them and ask their forgiveness as soon as possible. As you guide and strengthen me, I will go."

Giving Forgiveness

> For if you forgive men their trespasses, your heavenly Father will also forgive you. But if you do not forgive men their trespasses, neither will your Father forgive your trespasses. (Matt. 6:14–15, KJV)

Explanation: In prayer, there is a connection between what God does and what you do. You can't get forgiveness from God, for instance, without also forgiving others. If you refuse to do your part, you cut yourself off from God's part.

Dear God, I choose to forgive [name the person you feel has offended you in some way or toward whom you feel a bitterness and name the specific thing that prompted you to be angry, offended, or bitter].

Note: This might even be God himself. Yes, you might be angry at God. Be specific. Name the person and the offense below.

_____

_____

_____

_____

_____

_____

Pray: "Help me to see the greatness in him or her and to love him or her the way that You do. Help me to relinquish the anger that I'm experiencing so that I can walk in the fruit of love, joy, peace, patience, kindness, goodness, faithfulness, gentleness, and self-control. Help me to heal from this incident and to release any bitterness that I may be harboring. Please give me guidance in this situation, Holy Spirit, so that I can approach it in the way that is most pleasing to You. Help me, God, to do Your will. Thank You, and in Jesus's mighty name, I pray. Amen."

You may need to use this "prayer agenda" over and over as God brings up things from the past that you need to talk over with the Lord. But keep this promise in mind and repeat it back to God when your mind seems to be filled with terrible thoughts. Those with a bipolar disorder will experience this sort of thing from time to time.

Romans 8:1 says, "There is therefore now no condemnation to those who are in Christ Jesus, who do not walk according to the flesh, but according to the Spirit" (NKJV).

Warning: If You are holding on to an unforgiving spirit toward someone and they are unaware of it, *please* do not go to them and open an unnecessary wound. Handle it between you and God.

9

RECLEANSING YOUR HEART

Hebrews 10:22 says, "Let us draw near with a true heart in full assurance of faith, our hearts sprinkled clean from an evil conscience and our bodies washed in pure water."

Our relationship with the Lord always begins and is maintained through our heart. Our heart is the gateway of our whole being. So what we open our heart to determines what we let into our inner being. We were created by God with a spirit to receive and contain His life and with a heart to love Him. The condition of our heart is extremely important. In fact, many problems in our Christian life are really "heart problems."

The Greek word for heart is *kardia* and is the word from where we get "cardiac," and it refers to the physical blood pump in our bodies that is necessary to physical life. It is the spiritual heart to which the New Testament refers, and it is necessary to spiritual life.

The word *heart* in Scripture can be described as

- the seat of our affection;
- the seat of our motives and actions;
- the control center of our mind, will, and emotions; and
- the center of our entire personality.

In the following scriptures, we can see that the spiritual condition of an individual reflects the spiritual condition of the heart:

- Guard your heart above all else, for it is the source of life. (Prov. 4:23)
- Be angry and do not sin; on your bed, reflect in your heart and be still. (Ps. 4:4)
- A good man produces good out of the good storeroom of his heart. An evil man produces evil out of the evil storeroom, for his mouth speaks from the overflow of the heart. (Luke 6:45)
- One believes with the heart, resulting in righteousness, and one confesses with the mouth, resulting in salvation. (Rom. 10:10)

The heart always works from the inside out. When the heart is right on the inside, the actions will be right on the outside.

Jesus taught in the Sermon on the Mount that he wanted His children to have a pure heart, a heart that has been cleansed and recleansed: "The pure in heart are blessed, for they will see God" (Matt. 5:8).

To be pure in heart is to be rid of fears, tensions, and problems by admitting them and dealing with them. Jesus is talking about a heart that has been purged, cleansed, refined, and purified. He is also referring to a heart that is honest and has no hidden motives.

Naturally, without Christ, we have a heart that cannot be trusted. The old nature cannot be trusted. Christ gives us a new nature when we trust Christ to change us from the inside out. He gives us a new heart. The following scripture indicates the need for a new heart (a new spiritual heart): "Therefore, if anyone is in Christ, he is a new creation; old things have passed away, and look, new things have come" (2 Cor. 5:17).

Let me interject a personal illustration at this point. Earlier in this book, I mentioned a Christian psychiatrist Marie and I met when we were serving a church in Oregon. Dr. JR had a tremendous testimony of how he came to know Christ as his personal savior. He had been in general medical practice for several years. He indicated many of the individuals he was treating had problems that could not be addressed by a simple prescription. He was talking about mental, emotional, psychosomatic problems, etc. So he went back to school and became a psychiatrist.

At that time, he was not a practicing Christian. According to his own account, having a scientific mind-set and keeping accurate notes, he began to observe an interesting phenomenon. His patients who claimed to be Christians (sincere ones) showed higher rates of improvement in their conditions, and their improvement seemed to come more quickly. This started him on a quest that ultimately led to his conversion to Christ.

Do I believe that one must be a Christian to deal with the problem of depression, a bipolar condition, or any one of dozens of other mental or psychological problems? No. But I do believe the best answers for long-term help can only come when we get to know the "Maker" of the equipment. Even an old Buick I drove for a few years had an owner's manual written by the manufacturer. By the way, I did not blame General Motors for defective parts after 200,000 miles and a lot of rough treatment. It was not built to last forever. Now, because of the sin that our first parents, Adam and Eve, brought into the world and the kind of treatment we put our bodies through, it's a wonder we last as long as we do.

We are kept clean by the Word of God. Note the following scripture: "How can a young man keep his way pure? By keeping Your word. I have sought You with all my heart; don't let me wander from Your commands" (Ps. 119:9–10).

Finally, Jesus says the "pure in heart will see God." I think He is referring to more than heaven after this life has ended. I believe Jesus is speaking of our intimate experience with Him now. We can see God in His word (see the aforementioned scripture), and we can see God in His creation: "The heavens declare the glory of God, and the sky proclaims the work of His hands" (Ps. 19:1).

We do have to have our spiritual eyes open. There is a story told of three men standing on the edge of the Grand Canyon. One was an artist who had lost his faith in any religion many years earlier in his life. One was an old, rough cowboy who had not been to church in thirty years. The third one was a Christian who had just returned from a prayer retreat in the mountains.

The artist said, "What a picture!"

The cowboy said, "What an awful place to lose a cow!"

The Christian said, "What hath God wrought!"

My daddy used to say to me, "We believe in a heartfelt faith." One old preacher used to advise me to preach to folk's hearts, not just their heads. Then he would say, "Everybody has a heart, but not everybody has a head." In these days of spiritual darkness, it is hard to see that everybody has a heart. But they do, yet it is often the kind of heart the Bible describes as wicked and deceitful. Yet God the Holy Spirit can penetrate the hardest of hearts.

Over and over again Jesus would repeat the phrase *"He who has ears to hear, let him hear."* Many years ago, as a boy, I watched the television show *Dragnet*. Most of you reading this book have probably never heard of it. Jack Webb and Harry Morgan played the role of detectives in Los Angeles in the 1960s. Jack Webb, who starred as Sergeant Friday, would interview ladies, searching for information about a crime. His classic line was, "All we want is the facts, ma'am, just the facts."

Our problem today is, we are not even interested in the facts. We have completely forgotten how to listen with our heart. When we listen to our children's problems, we need to listen with our heart. When we communicate as husbands and wives, we need to listen with our hearts. When we read the scripture, we need to listen with our heart. We, as believers, need to make sure our hears are cleansed and recleansed so we can hear with our heart.

10

RENEWING YOUR MIND

Soul, translated as *psuche* in Greek and *Nephesh* in Hebrew, is the life principle of an individual. We are not a body with a soul; rather, we are a soul with a body. Since I have dealt with my diagnosis, I have become more keenly aware of how important Paul's instructions were concerning how to live above our circumstance and not under them. At the core of the soul is the mind, the emotions, and the will.

We must cooperate with God in the renewing of our mind. The mind is the seat of intellect, reasoning, forethought, judgment, and spiritual insight. The renewing of the mind results in several outcomes.

1. *The mind is transformed.*

I assure you, when the Scripture speaks of the mind, it is referring to more than the physical organ we call the brain. Paul says that our mind is renewed that it might be *transformed*, emphasizing, "Be transformed by the renewing of your mind, so that you may discern what is the good, pleasing, and perfect will of God" (Rom. 12:2).

The word *transformed* in the Greek is the word we use for a caterpillar becoming a butterfly—"metamorphosis." There is a spiritual symbiosis or linkage between the heart and mind. Sometimes in the Scripture, the words are used interchangeably, although there is a definable difference. A caterpillar turns to a butterfly from the design within, not from pressure without. So it is the same with a believer.

I was a guest speaker at a pastor's conference some years ago in Bangladesh. One of the gifts I received was a beautiful picture made entirely from butterfly wings. It was hard to imagine that those intricate, multicolored, beautiful wings were at one time caterpillars, worms. What an expression of God's plans and flawless design! The only way we as His children can be an expression of His plan, design, and will is through having our minds transformed by His direction.

You can read books, earn scholarly degrees, and be trained by the best practitioners in what subject matter or skill you seek to master; but your mind will not be renewed. The renewing of the mind is God working from the inside out. You can cooperate with God and see His work proceed in a timely manner or you can hinder His working and become a believer confused in mind and heart.

All you allow in through the body gates, the Spirit of God must deal with. What you read, what you watch, what you listen to, what you put into your body are either a help to mind renewal or a hindrance to mind renewal.

I have discovered, for me, to get a good night's sleep, I need to carefully filter what comes through the body gates at least thirty minutes before I go to bed—no television, no internet, no emotionally elevated stimuli, either good or bad. I usually listen to soft worship music or some type of easy listening instrumental. I use aroma therapy during the night. We have a scent diffuser into which we put a few drops of essential oil. My wife and I prefer lavender, but there are hundreds to choose from.

2.   *The mind is informed.*

Another result of the mind being renewed is that it will be *informed*, as what is stated in Second Timothy 3:16–17:

> All Scripture is inspired by God and is profitable
> for teaching, for rebuking, for correcting, for
> training in righteousness, so that the man of God
> may be complete, equipped for every good work.

King David said that he would hide God's Word in his heart. There he was using the word *heart* and linking it with his mind. He was talking about memorizing Scripture—at least, if not word for word, the basic truth.

God's goal is for us to know God's perfect will for us by knowing

- what to believe, which is where the *teaching* is involved;
- what not to believe, where the *rebuking* is involved;
- what not to be doing, where the *correcting* takes place; and
- what to be doing, where the *training* comes in.

Go wants us to have a *spiritually mature mind equipped to meet any situation.*

3.   *The mind is conformed.*

The third result of the mind being renewed is that it will be *conformed* in harmony with our Lord Jesus, and our decisions will be steadfast based upon the wisdom we receive from the Father God. As we read in the Word,

> If any of you lack wisdom, let him ask of God, that giveth to all men liberally, and upbraideth not; and it shall be given him.
>
> But let him ask in faith, nothing wavering. For he that wavereth is like a wave of the sea driven with the wind and tossed.
>
> For let not that man think that he shall receive any thing of the Lord.
>
> A double minded man is unstable in all his ways. (Jam. 1:5–8, KJV)
>
> But if any of you needs wisdom, you should ask God for it. He is generous to everyone and will give you wisdom without criticizing you. But when you ask God, you must believe and not

doubt. Anyone who doubts is like a wave in the sea, blown up and down by the wind. Such doubters are thinking two different things at the same time, and they cannot decide about anything they do. They should not think they will receive anything from the Lord. (Jam. 1:5–8, NCV)

Notice that the New Century Version reveals that the "double-minded person" is one who has a hard time deciding.

One of the symptoms of a bipolar condition is the difficulty in making decisions. It seemed that simple decisions became increasingly difficult for me. I asked one of my godly counselors about the problems I was having in making what seemed to be the simplest of decisions. He wrote on a white board these four words and a short definition beside them:

- Genocide—the killing of a whole race of people
- Homicide—the killing of another person
- Suicide—killing yourself
- Decide—killing any other option

God has not given us the spirit of fear, but sometimes we allow an evil spirit to grip us with fear even when making small decisions because we are afraid we might make the wrong one and we cannot go back. My counselor suggested that the problem with decision-making is often brought about by fear. God does not give us the spirit of fear; He gives us the spirit of power, love, and a sound mind.

Paul tells us in 2 Timothy 1:7, "For God has not given us a spirit of fear, but of power and of love and of a sound mind" (NKJV). In the New Century Version, this reads as "For God has not given us a spirit of fearfulness, but one of power, love, and sound judgment."

I feel we could translate the latter part of verse 7 as "power, love, and a balanced mind."

4.   *The mind is battle formed.*

We read this in the Word:

> Finally, be strengthened by the Lord and by His vast strength. *Put on* the full armor of God so that you can *stand* against the tactics of the Devil. For our battle is not against flesh and blood, but against the rulers, against the authorities, against the world powers of this darkness, against the spiritual forces of evil in the heavens. This is why you must take up the full armor of God, so that you may be able to *resist* in the evil day, and having prepared everything, to take your stand. Stand, therefore, with truth like a belt around your waist, righteousness like armor on your chest, and your feet sandaled with readiness for the gospel of peace. In every situation take the shield of faith, and with it you will be able to *extinguish* all the flaming arrows of the evil one. Take the helmet of salvation, and the sword of the Spirit, which is God's word.
>
> *Pray* at all times in the Spirit with every prayer and request, and *stay alert* in this with all perseverance and intercession for all the saints. Pray also for me, that the message may be given to me when I open my mouth to make known with boldness the mystery of the gospel. For this I am an ambassador in chains. Pray that I might be bold enough in Him to speak as I should. (Eph. 6:10–20, author's italics)

Paul tells us that we are in a spiritual battle, not a physical one, and the weapons we use are spiritual weapons. The battle is won or lost in the mind. Paul also says in Second Corinthians 10:3–6 that

> for though we walk in the flesh, we do not war according to the flesh. For the weapons of our warfare are not carnal but mighty in God for pulling down strongholds, casting down arguments and every high thing that exalts itself against the knowledge of God, bringing every thought into captivity to the obedience of Christ, and being ready to punish all disobedience when your obedience is fulfilled.

So how is the mind battle formed?

1. *Preparation.* Preparation is made by *putting on* the complete armor of God. Notice the helmet of salvation and the sword of the spirit. These are the two most vital parts of the armor. It is the "helmet of salvation," indicating that from our relationship with Christ, everything else flows. It is a head covering, representing the mind where the battle is won or lost.

2. *Position.* Your position is one of *standing.* As a soldier of the cross, the victory has already been won through the cross and the resurrection. We are standing in Christ's victory. It is tragic the amount of time and effort believers waste trying to win a battle that has already been won. Christ has already been declared the victor. Praise His dear name!

3. *Prevention.* The key word in verse 13 is resist. We have been given the delegated authority and power of our Lord to resist any advance of the enemy into the believer's camp.

4. *Purge.* We can purge or extinguish the flaming arrows (the lies against the truth thrown at us by Satan) by the shield of faith. Our faith will be tested, but we must believe in the

truth of God over the lies of the world and the evil one. God gives us clarity of mind to know the truth.

5. *Prayer.* I have come to believe that what the devil fears most from a child of God is not their church attendance, their Bible reading, or even their witnessing as important as those things are. What he fears most is a believer on their knees, and with a broken heart and a mind set on things above, bombarding heaven with their prayers. The angels sing, Christ rejoices, God the Father is glorified, the Holy Spirit acts, demons stop up their ears, and someone's life is changed. And Satan cannot do a thing about it.

6. *Perceptiveness.* The key word is alert. God prepares our minds by making us alert to the tactics or our enemy. He hones our minds to be spiritually sharp.

11

REDIRECTING YOUR EMOTIONS

I heard an evangelist tell a church he was preaching to say, "Israel was God's chosen race, but I honestly believe I have found in this church God's 'frozen race.'" Needless to say, that comment did not get a lot of amens. Of course, he did not expect it would. But by the time he had finished his message, the congregation had begun to understand the preacher's burden.

I have been in some of those churches where I felt a cold draft rather than a warm welcome. I have been around those who claim to be believers who gave me more of a cold blast than a Christian blessing. It was a chill, but not a thrill. Some of them, bless their heart, showed about as much emotion toward their faith as a wax statue. I am not talking about emotionalism. As one country philosopher said, most "-isms" ought to be "wuz-ums."

The fact is, we are emotional beings. Our soul (psuche in Greek) is made up of mind, emotions, and will. We come now to discuss the emotional part of our soul. The emotional part of our soul includes love, hatred, joy, and grief. The Word in the Song of Solomon says,

> Tell me, you, the one I love: Where do you pasture your sheep? Where do you let them rest at noon? Why should I be like one who veils herself beside the flocks of your companions? (1:7)

Psalm 42:1 follows the same message: "As a deer longs for streams of water, so I long for You, God."

The forgoing verses show us that to love is a function of the emotional part of the soul. The following verses show us that hating, loathing, and despising are also in the soul. Despising in the soul is the hatred of the soul.

- "They loathed all food and came near the gates of death." (Ps. 107:18)
- "This is what the Lord GOD says: Certainly, in My burning zeal I speak against the rest of the nations and all of Edom, who took My land as their own possession with wholehearted rejoicing and utter contempt so that its pastureland became plunder." (Ezek. 36:5)

Joy is a great part of the emotion. These verses beam a certain joy found only in the Lord:

- "I greatly rejoice in the LORD, I exult in my God." (Isa. 61:10)
- "Bring joy to Your servant's life, because I turn to You, Lord." (Ps. 86:4)
- "You may spend the money on anything you want: cattle, sheep, wine, beer, or anything you desire. You are to feast there in the presence of the LORD your God and rejoice with your family." (Deut. 14:26)

On a practical level, I have learned to redirect my emotions. Living with a bipolar condition, you realize that your emotions are super sensitive. For me I cannot even watch a favorite football team play, especially if the score is close. That may seem odd to some folks, but it can literally throw my emotions completely out of balance. It does not matter if these are good emotions.

I must be very careful about attending funerals and funeral visitations. I have watched certain movies (good movies) but had to stop watching them because I was becoming too emotional. I love to listen to great Gospel music but often must take a break because of crying spells.

Not everyone is put together the same way, but my bipolar has seemed to heighten my emotional experiences, so I must redirect my emotions into other things. In other words, I need to control my emotions and not let my emotions control me. What I am advising is to learn to let your emotions be a natural part of who you are. Express your emotions in love for one another in appropriate ways. Use your emotions to appropriately praise and worship God. But know when to slow down and put on the brakes.

12

RETRAINING YOUR WILL

When God created mankind, Scripture declares that He made us in His image. Among other things, that means we have the ability to choose. Our heart, which is the core of our soul or life, expresses itself through our mind, our emotions, and our will or ability to choose. Jesus expresses that in the following verse:

> Anyone who chooses to do the will of God will find out whether my teaching comes from God or whether I speak on my own. (John 7:17, NIV)

Making choices is not always an easy thing to do. I have already dealt with the reasons why it might be difficult. Once choices are made, we often find even greater difficulty in carrying through with those choices. Paul deals realistically with that problem in the Book of Romans:

> For we know that the law is spiritual, but I am made out of flesh, sold into sin's power. For I do not understand what I am doing, because I do not practice what I want to do, but I do what I hate. And if I do what I do not want to do, I agree with the law that it is good. So now I am no longer the one doing it, but it is sin living in me. For I know that nothing good lives in me, that is, in my flesh. For the desire to do what is good is with me, but

there is no ability to do it. For I do not do the good that I want to do, but I practice the evil that I do not want to do. Now if I do what I do not want, I am no longer the one doing it, but it is the sin that lives in me. So I discover this principle: When I want to do what is good, evil is with me. For in my inner self I joyfully agree with God's law. But I see a different law in the parts of my body, waging war against the law of my mind and taking me prisoner to the law of sin in the parts of my body. What a wretched man I am! Who will rescue me from this dying body? I thank God through Jesus Christ our Lord! So then, with my mind I myself am a slave to the law of God, but with my flesh, to the law of sin. (Rom. 6:14–25)

If Paul can acknowledge that it takes divine power to live out the Christian faith, even after the right decision is made, then certainly we who deal with emotional, psychological, or mental thorns must recognize that the Christian life is not hard to live—it is impossible! It is impossible without the power of a resurrected Lord. Perhaps in verse 25 of the aforementioned passage, Paul was thinking about the Roman practice of sometimes hanging the dead body around the neck of the one who killed them. This would be their punishment as they had to put up with the stench, flies, dogs, and all the shame that went it. Paul is saying, "Spiritually, I can be daily rescued from this dead or dying body through Jesus Christ." We have this same hope.

Because we have a will, we can choose to have a Christian family. We can be like Joshua, as we read in the following verse:

But if it doesn't please you to worship Yahweh, choose for yourselves today the one you will worship: the gods your fathers worshiped beyond the Euphrates River or the gods of the Amorites in whose land you are living. As for me and my family, we will worship Yahweh. (Josh. 4:15)

Because we have a will, we can refuse to bow down to political correctness. The Hebrew children had a choice, and though it could have cost them their lives, they chose correctly. This we read in the Book of Daniel:

> Shadrach, Meshach, and Abednego replied to the king, "Nebuchadnezzar, we don't need to give you an answer to this question. If the God we serve exists, then He can rescue us from the furnace of blazing fire, and He can rescue us from the power of you, the king. But even if He does not rescue us, we want you as king to know that we will not serve your gods or worship the gold statue you set up." (Dan. 3:16–18)

Because we can choose, we have the right and obligation to share our faith to those we love, as the Acts of the Apostles teaches us:

> So they called for them and ordered them not to preach or teach at all in the name of Jesus.
> But Peter and John answered them, "Whether it's right in the sight of God for us to listen to you rather than to God, you decide; for we are unable to stop speaking about what we have seen and heard." (Acts 4:18–20)

So how do you re-train your will? Here are six things you need to do:

1. *You need to know the facts involved in the decision you are about to make.* As an example, I will use an upcoming mission trip to Suriname. Before I said *yes* to making the trip, I needed to know the general time frame and in general what we would be expected to do.

2. *You need to have in mind what the next step would be.* In my case, it would be to know the exact date, the cost, and more about the work we would be doing while there.

3. *You need to help your will to "will."* For me, this involves being prepared spiritually, writing myself notes, and reading and meditating on encouraging devotionals. Also, it means corresponding with the missionaries.

4. *You need to dwell on positive outcomes of previous good choices.* For me, this would include the last trip to Suriname, as well as many other mission trips that I have taken. It is not that those trips were free of snags, but I always dwell on the joyous, blessed outcomes of those trips. The time and effort we put into them was worth it all. That encourages my will.

5. *Be consistent.* I have found that being consistent is one of the best ways to retrain my will to match God's will. Scripture declares that God is the same, yesterday, today, and tomorrow. His love and compassion never changes. What I will should always be consistent. Whether I am up or down, what I will should reflect my connection with the Father, not my temporary psychological or emotional symptom. Sometimes that is not an easy task, but it is my goal and it should be your goal.

6. *Finally, never give up.* If you are completely sure the Lord was behind your decision, stick with it.

Warning: Make sure your decision was not a result of a manic or a depression episode. Turn to your friends and those who are holding you accountable for their advice.

But if you are certain you are on the right track, stick it out, trust God, and continue in the direction you are going until you hear something different from the Lord.

13

REPAIRING YOUR BODY

During the '70s when I was attending the Mid-America Baptist Seminary in Memphis, Tennessee, a professor in pastoral ministry class had us young pastors write a paper on "Temple Maintenance." He had spent some time talking to us about the importance of taking care of our bodies. He talked about proper rest, a good diet, and a sufficient amount of regular exercise. Our paper was to include a possible schedule and proposed routine that would result in good temple maintenance. I think I received an A on the paper. But I am ashamed to say, I flunked the follow-through. I am afraid I was not the only one who had trouble with the follow-through. Good intentions are not enough to keep us healthy.

With God, there is no harsh dividing line between the physical and the spiritual. All that we are and all that we do intersect with the spiritual. The Scripture declares in First Corinthians 10:31, "Therefore, whether you eat or drink, or whatever you do, do everything for God's glory."

I remember attending a conference with Marie and several couples from Illinois at what was then a church in Florida where Dr. Peter Lord was pastoring. It was a wonderful retreat. I remember Brother Lord asking us in one session how many spiritual things we had done that day.

A few hands went up, and upon asking them the number of spiritual things they had done—some rather embarrassingly would say one, or maybe two, and, at the most, three. They were thinking about their morning devotional or maybe a kind word they said to a friend or to their spouse.

Then Brother Lord asked, "How many of you brushed your teeth this morning?" Every hand went up. Then he said, "Is brushing your teeth a nonspiritual activity?" He reminded us that the Scripture says that "whether we eat or drink or whatever we do we are to do it to the glory of God" (1 Cor. 10:31). He indicated that somehow, we have gotten confused between a spiritual activity and a religious activity. "All we do is spiritual if it fits into God's overall plan for our lives," Dr. Lord emphasized.

Physical exercise or activity is spiritual, if that is God's plan for you. And beyond that, it reminds us of this body that God created. Just to analyze it gives glory to God. I have a paper written by a pastor friend, Dr. Tim Adams, who I was in seminary with and have helped in numerous Evangelistic meetings. Our body is an example of the spiritual genius of God.

The Human Machine

> I will praise thee; for I am fearfully and wonder-
> fully made marvelous are thy works; and that my
> soul knoweth right well. (Ps. 139:14)

The human machine is a seven-part miracle machine of creation:

- About 200–212 I-beams, angle, U-joint-type material called bone built to withstand several pounds of pressure.
- All 14 types of mechanical, motorized, electrically generated aids to ambulation in all directions.
- An unbelievable 1000s of miles of expandable state-of-the-art, lead-resistant plumbing, half with dependable one-way valves, connected to a super pump in miniature model built for 24-hour service, maintaining constant respiration, nourishment, disposal, and cosmetic functions thru circulation of 4 quarts of lubricant/cleaner at the rate of 70–80 BPM.

- An internal waste management system comprised of one self-emptying storage tank for liquid disposal and 27 feet of absorptive lining for the transport and expulsion of semi-solid waste.
- A four-part equalized chemical-balance injection system built to lifetime automatic revisions in the human model without need for recall to the factory.
- A microscopically integrated internal communication network connected to a central receiving and response station far outranking the complexities of any computerized, modern metropolitan live informational transfer and recording system.
- All neatly wrapped in two layers of the toughest, thermal, protective, regenerating covering called skin.

The human machine retail price—$$$ Priceless.

The Word declares that when God breathed into man's nostrils His breath, man became a spiritual being. That extended to woman as well. Paul says in First Corinthians 6:19–20, "Don't you know that your body is a sanctuary of the Holy Spirit who is in you, whom you have from God? You are not your own, for you were bought at a price. Therefore, glorify God in your body."

For the true follower of Christ, the concept that Paul teaches is not a difficult one. It means very simply that our bodies belong to God. They are indwelt by the Holy Spirit. We are caretakers, stewards, of this temple, this sanctuary in which God lives.

When God first created mankind, it was next to him in its wonder, ability, and brainpower. Man was not a little god, but he was the crowning act of God's earthly creation. Man and woman were to never be sick, or sad, or depressed, or experience anxiety, or die. But the entrance of sin changed all that. Now we must work with an imperfect body in an imperfect world and do what we can to stay as healthy as possible.

My Experience

It was the fall of 2015 and Marie and I had just celebrated our fiftieth wedding anniversary in June of that year. In the spring, we were planning a trip to Europe to be with our son-in-law, daughter, and our two granddaughters, where Joey was stationed on an army base in Germany. It was a kind of anniversary trip.

I was dealing with my bipolar condition; but beside that, I was overweight, had type II diabetes, acid reflux, high cholesterol, high blood pressure, and was totally out of shape physically, especially for the type of walking I knew we would be doing. Well, with what I believe was direction from the Lord, I decided to become a different person physically by the time we left for Europe in March 2016.

With encouragement from Marie and direction from a great doctor (Thank you, Dr. Simon), even including days of Thanksgiving and Christmas, I

- lost approximately forty pounds;
- was completely free of acid reflux;
- had no more diabetes II or need to take any drug;
- markedly lowered my cholesterol;
- controlled my blood pressure;
- was exercising regularly five times a week for at least thirty minutes per day;
- felt better emotionally, mentally, and physically; and
- was no longer considered obese.

I continued the program after I returned to the States. After I reached my weight goal, I went on the maintenance part of the program. At the time I went through it, Dr. Rebecca Simon was a licensed practitioner of the Physicians' Medical Weight Loss Program. One of the things that helped me was to keep a daily log of my food intake and my daily exercise.

One day in discussing my situation with Dr. Rebecca, I asked her a rather dumb question.

"Does exercise help relieve depression?"

"Sure it does!" she answered.

Well, I knew that. The illustration I gave earlier about man being a miracle machine has just one problem—man is more than a machine. We are an organic life containing work of an almighty God. We have within us God's breath and the spark of His Deity. No machine, however refined or complicated, can have that. Oh yes, medical science has advanced to the point where we can get spare parts from other bodies when they expire. We can make artificial limbs and even blood pumps. But we cannot create life. And when mankind thinks he has, God will surely have a big surprise for him.

The truth is, we have one body and we are responsible for taking care of it. We are not to worship it as some of the ancient Greeks and Romans did and as many in Hollywood and the Western culture do today. We are not to sacrifice it to dark religions as hundreds in the past have done and some do today. Nor are we to destroy it with hedonistic practices and appetites of demons. We are to honor God with it and present it to Him as a living sacrifice.

Let me conclude this chapter by suggesting some practical biblical ways we can repair the body:

1. *Rest.* Keep the Sabbath. The Bible says that God created the world in six days and rested on the seventh day. God did not need the rest, but He knew that man would need it. The Sabbath became a special day for the Hebrews, even before the Ten Commandments were given. "Sabbath" does not mean "seventh"; it means "rest." Today, that commandment is probably the most violated and the least understood of all the commandments. It has less to do with a particular day than it does with what we do with one out of seven days. Notice the words in Exodus 20:8–11:

   > Remember the Sabbath day, to keep it holy: You are to labor six days and do all your work, but the seventh day is a Sabbath to the LORD your God. You must not do any work—you, your son or daughter, your male or female slave, your live-

> stock, or the foreigner who is within your gates.
> For the LORD made the heavens and the earth,
> the sea, and everything in them in six days; then
> He rested on the seventh day. Therefore the LORD
> blessed the Sabbath day and declared it holy.

The need for rest was placed in mankind's DNA by our creator. It was put there even before we fell into sin. We were to work, which was never a curse, and then we were to rest. I think that worship was something we were to practice every day.

For many people, Sunday is not a Sabbath, especially for pastors. Sunday is often our busiest day. For the Jewish rabbi, the Sabbath is his busiest day; but it is not his personal Sabbath. What I am saying is very simple—we need to take a sabbath (with a small *s*). If we do not rest, we are breaking the spirit of that Commandment.

2. *Sleeping well.* Probably about 8 hours.
3. *Letting the brain rest awhile.* No news, no junk, no politics, etc.
4. *Practicing positive meditation.* The Bible teaches us this in Philippians 4:8: "Finally brothers, whatever is true, whatever is honorable, whatever is just, whatever is pure, whatever is lovely, whatever is commendable—if there is any moral excellence and if there is any praise—dwell on these things."
5. *Adopting a hobby.* Preferably one that takes you out doors where you can breathe some fresh air.
6. *Not poisoning your body.* Do not eat it, inhale it, smoke it, drink it, or inject it if you know it harms your body. First Corinthians 6:19–20 says,

> Don't you know that your body is a sanctuary of
> the Holy Spirit who is in you, whom you have from
> God? You are not your own, for you were bought at
> a price. Therefore glorify God in your body.

7. *Eating well-balanced meals.* Before the Great Flood of Noah, according to scripture, mankind was vegetarian. After the flood,

God included meat for his diet. The New Testament has this to say: "Therefore, whether you eat or drink, or whatever you do, do everything for God's glory" (1 Cor. 10:31). I will not go into detail, but I try to have a balance of meat, vegetables, and fruits. I try to watch my calories and carbs. I am still working to get my sugar back under control. I was there about two years past, and I will be there again. It takes some self-control.

8. *Drinking plenty of water.* About eight glasses a day.

9. *Getting sufficient exercise.* We do not all need to be athletes or spend hours a day in the gym. We simply need to be active. Do not sit so much. Do some form of mild cardio and exercise on a regular basis. Try walking thirty minutes a day, five days a week.

   Often scientists tell us that through evolution, man has gained the "fight or flight" response. I believe God put that in Man's DNA at creation, which we can read in Genesis 1:8: "God blessed them, and God said to them, 'Be fruitful, multiply, fill the earth, and subdue it. Rule the fish of the sea, the birds of the sky, and every creature that crawls on the earth.'"

   It would take a very healthy individual pair to rule over the earth. Mankind surely needed the so-called "fight or flight" response in dealing with the animal kingdom, even though their nature had not been altered by the introduction of sin.

10. *Finding a good doctor.* Everyone needs a doctor they can trust—that is, has a willingness to talk and answer questions and treat you in a holistic way. By that, I mean someone who respects and understands you not just from a physical point of view but from a psychological and spiritual point of view.

11. *Finally, if you need medicine, take it.* This is especially taught to us in First Timothy 5:23: "Don't continue drinking only water, but use a little wine because of your stomach and your frequent illnesses."

    Luke, who was a physician, traveled with Paul on many of his missionary journeys. It seems he had learned from Dr. Luke the medicinal value of wine. Apparently, Timothy, who would later join Paul, had some form of stomach problem. We see in the mentioned verse, Paul giving young Timothy a suggestion about how he might treat his ailing stomach.

Remember these:

1. It is much better to stay well than to treat the sickness that may result from not doing what is necessary to stay well. One reason I like my doctor so much is that she majors on wellness.
2. If possible, I prefer being treated with natural medicines rather than synthetic drugs. I know this is not always possible.

There are several things that help make my bipolar condition manageable. One of those things is medicine. I could use the word *drugs*, but I like the sound of *medicine* better. I guess the reason is because there is so much misuse, overuse, and illegal use attached to the word *drugs*. It sounds better even though there is no difference. A drug can kill you or save your life. There is nothing wrong with taking the proper medicine in the proper dosage, for the proper reason, at the proper times. And one must never stop taking those prescribed medicines without the doctor's approval and guidance.

14
POSTSCRIPTS

I felt that I had completed my portion of this book until a recent Sunday. Speaking at our church (First Baptist, Harrison, Arkansas) was Jamie Womack from Louisiana. She has had a disability from birth that could have kept her from achieving any level of success. But instead, God has used her disability and turned it into an advantage for His glory.

As I listened to her testimony, I realized there was one thing I had not done that often resulted in a round of depression. Jamie said she learned to embrace her disability instead of complaining about it. God spoke to my heart, "*You must stop complaining about your bipolar weaknesses and begin to embrace your condition.*" Right then and there, I surrendered myself to Christ in that regard. The Word is clear:

> Therefore, so that I would not exalt myself, a thorn in the flesh was given to me, a messenger of Satan to torment me so I would not exalt myself. Concerning this, I pleaded with the Lord three times to take it away from me. But He said to me, "My grace is sufficient for you, for power is perfected in weakness." Therefore, I will most gladly boast all the more about my weaknesses, so that Christ's power may reside in me. So I take pleasure in weaknesses, insults, catastrophes, persecutions, and in pressures, because of Christ. For when I am weak, then I am strong. (2 Cor. 12:7–10)

Now we have this treasure in clay jars, so that this extraordinary power may be from God and not from us. We are pressured in every way but not crushed; we are perplexed but not in despair; we are persecuted but not abandoned; we are struck down but not destroyed. We always carry the death of Jesus in our body, so that the life of Jesus may also be revealed in our body. For we who live are always given over to death because of Jesus, so that Jesus' life may also be revealed in our mortal flesh. (2 Cor. 4:7–11)

If Paul could go from the "chief of sinners" to one who had to live with a thorn in his flesh day and night, face persecution, insults, live under the threat of death, and yet take pleasure in it for the sake of Christ his Lord—who am I to question his wisdom? The happiest, most spiritual people I have known are those who are beset with physical or psychological malady.

Lord, do what you will with this house of clay, that the light of your presence within may shine through. I challenge you, the reader, know that your life is a temple meant to be indwelt by the Lord Jesus Christ. He is to be seated upon the throne of your life, to rule and reign. He comes in by invitation and rules by your submission. The temple does not have to be perfect, beautiful, or even well-constructed. It simply needs to be under the control of Christ the Lord. Make it so!

REFERENCES

Culhane, Dennis. "Five Myths about America's Homeless." The Washington Post. WP Company, July 11, 2010. http://www.washingtonpost.com/wp-dyn/content/article/2010/07/09/AR2010070902357.html.

Diagnostic and Statistical Manual of Mental Disorders. London: American Psychiatric Association, 2013.

Hutchcraft, Ron. "A Word with You, Daily Devotional." *A Word with You, Daily Devotional* (blog), n.d.

Moran, Lord. *Winston Churchill: The Struggle for Survival.* Houghton Mifflin, 1966.

Ridgaway, Toni. "Silent Suffering: Pastors and Depression." *USA Today*, September 11, 2010.

Ross, Sky Lea. "6 Wrong Assumptions People Make about Mental Illness and the Truth They Need to Know." Thought Catalog, May 26, 2016. https://thoughtcatalog.com/sky-lea-ross/2016/05/6-wrong-assumptions-people-make-about-mental-illness-and-the-truth-they-need-to-know.

Shenk, Joshua Wolf. "Lincoln's Great Depression." The Atlantic. Atlantic Media Company, October 1, 2005. http://www.theatlantic.com/magazine/archive/2005/10/lincolns-great-depression/304247.

Spurgeon, C. H. *Letters to My Students.* Vol. 1. Zondervan, 1954.

Recommendations/ Endorsements for The Elijah Syndrome

This was a great investment of time and emotion. It will prove to be a great help to those afflicted with bipolar syndrome and with those who work with or care for them. One of the great values of your book is that you explain issues in everyday terms so that a nonmedical person can grasp what is being said.

—Don Moore, BA, ThM, DD
Retired executive director
Arkansas Baptist State Convention

I minister to depressed, burned out, and discouraged pastors every week, so I was excited to get a copy of *The Elijah Syndrome*. I now have another good resource to put in the hands of hurting ministers. The author speaks in a straightforward yet compassionate manner. His book not only helps individuals understand the problem but offers hope for people who may have lost hope. I highly recommend *The Elijah Syndrome* to every pastor!

—Dr. J. Marcus Merritt
Director of church minister relations
Georgia Baptist Mission Board

Ray Edwards and I have been friends since the summer of 1980. I have known of his ministry from a distance and found him to be a faithful minister of the gospel, demonstrating truthfulness, trustworthiness, and loyalty. It must be said that his wife, Marie, has been very instrumental to his life, work, and ministry.

In this book, Ray shows his humanity without ever blaming anyone for his mental illness. Truly amazing! I read it through tears and laughter. It should be required reading for all who want to better understand mental illness, particularly bipolar disorder. This book may be his finest work, and I highly recommend it.

May God use this work for the glory of Jesus.

Roger Williams, BS, MDiv, honorary doctorate
Retired pastor, Annville, Kentucky

I must say Ray's openness and insight will no doubt benefit many who wrestle with this issue. Every pastor, Christian counselor, and concerned believer will gain a wealth of understanding in ministering to others.

Delton Beall, BA, MDiv
State director, Florida Baptist Disaster Relief

Being aware of the journey he recounts in his writing, I can attest to its "blow-by-blow" accuracy and depth of experience. I believe it to be a vital resource to aid in the proper self-management by those with such conditions and understanding by those with whom they live or relate.

Dr. James D. Bryant, MDiv, DMin
Pastor, Gaither Baptist Church
Harrison, Arkansas

It is an honor for me to recommend *The Elijah Syndrome* written by my friend Raymond Edwards. Raymond is one of those guys you always look forward to seeing at church or denominational meetings. He is always so gracious, kind, and caring. When great man like Raymond shares his heart and his journey, I listen with intense reverence because of the respect I have for him.

Many of our leaders in ministry and church leadership struggle with similar borderline or full-blown emotional health issues. Legions of people in our churches live with, and minister to, family members who struggle with these issues. For the most part, these folks feel lonely, overwhelmed, and alone.

It is way past time that our churches understand and accept the reality of emotional and mental health issues and become incredibly proficient at recognizing and ministering in these situations.

Thank you, Raymond, for the boldness, transparency, and compassion required to share the contents of this book.

I highly recommend this book. I pray God will use it as a catalyst for quality and compassionate ministry in this oft neglected arena of real life.

J. D. "Sonny" Tucker, PhD
Executive director
Arkansas Baptist State Convention

7   Experiencing the Living God

[1] David French, "Watch Bernie Sanders Attack a Christian Nominee and Impose an Unconstitutional Religious Test for Public Office," National Review, June 7, 2017. http://www.nationalreview.com/corner/448393/watch-bernie-sanders-unconstitutionally-impose-religious-test-public-office.

About the Author

Raymond and Anna Marie grew up on small farms in northwest Arkansas. Their families were faithful followers of Christ and were active in small Baptist churches.

Raymond and Anna Marie were converted to Christ during their teen years. Raymond surrendered to the Gospel ministry when he was eighteen and married Anna Marie Estes when he was nineteen. Together they spent the next fifteen years pastoring and receiving their formal education.

Raymond has a bachelor of arts from Southwest Baptist University, Bolivar, Missouri, and a Master of Divinity (MDiv) from Southwestern Baptist Theological Seminary, Fort Worth, Texas. Anna Marie was able to complete a little over two years of college work.

After Approximately forty-five years of pastoring in various states, traveling to many countries to do mission work and spending twelve years as a college adjunct professor, Raymond was diagnosed with a bipolar condition. Since retiring from the pastorate and preaching ministry, Raymond spends much of his time writing Bible studies, articles of general interest, and poetry. He has a ministry called "Poetic Paraphrase."

Raymond and Marie are active members of First Baptist Church, Harrison, Arkansas. He is still able to participate in foreign mission activities. They enjoy two children and two college-age granddaughters.

CPSIA information can be obtained
at www.ICGtesting.com
Printed in the USA
FSHW020328200620
71367FS